D0145078

EARLY CHILDHOOD EDUCATION SERIES

Leslie R. Williams, Editor
Millie Almy, Senior Advisor

ADVISORY BOARD: **Barbara T. Bowman, Harriet K. Cuffaro, Stephanie Feeney, Doris Pronin Fromberg, Celia Genishi, Dominic F. Gullo, Alice Sterling Honig, Elizabeth Jones, Gwen Morgan, David Weikert**

(Continued)

Scenes From Day Care

How Teachers Teach and What Children Learn

ELIZABETH BALLIETT PLATT

Teachers College, Columbia University
New York and London

Published by Teachers College Press, 1234 Amsterdam Avenue
New York, NY 10027

Library of Congress Cataloging-in-Publication Data

Platt, Elizabeth Balliett.
    Scenes from day care : how teachers teach and what children learn
/ Elizabeth Balliett Platt.
    p.   cm. — (Early childhood education series)
Includes bibliographical references and index.
ISBN 0–8077–3131–5 (pbk.)
1. Day care centers—United States.   2. Education, Preschool—
United states.   I. Title.   II. Series.
HV854.P53   1991
362.7′12′0973—dc20   91–31286
                                                              CIP

Printed on acid-free paper

Manufactured in the United States of America

99 98 97 96 95 94 93 92 91   8 7 6 5 4 3 2 1

To
All the Children in Day Care
and
to John

Contents

Introduction
The Questions

By the end of the 20th century, if current trends continue, a large majority of children in the United States will be enrolled in some form of day care during all or part of their first 5 years. Given this kind of forecast, we have to assume that day care will have a transforming role in our society. It is the first time in history that a whole society has shifted from family care to group care in such enormous numbers. On a very large scale children and families in this generation, and the adults and families of the future, will be different because of it.

What are the long-term effects of this rush into group child care? How will the minds and behaviors of children growing up right now be changed by the day-care experiences we are providing for them? By looking in detail at what actually happens to children in specific situations, perhaps we can identify the kind of positives that we want to build on as well as the negatives we need to avoid or change in our children's day-care experience. The more we are able to understand the likely effects on children of this huge experiment, the better able we will be to influence how it will go.

We already have many excellent guidelines for planning and running good day-care programs. These have been carefully worked out by early childhood educators, based on what has been learned through both research and experience, about child care and child development. They spell out in detail what good care is and how we can provide it. Yet despite the studies, and conferences, and the books and manuals, all focused on ensuring quality group care for young children, the gap between theory and practice remains disturbingly wide in many centers. This is a frustrating state of affairs for parents, teachers, administrators, and everyone else who is concerned for the future.

If we think we know what quality care is, why can't we provide it with more consistency? Part of the answer is the lack of sufficient money to develop and administer the needed child-care services for infants, toddlers, and preschool children. But another part of the answer has to do with the inner content of programs, the style, the approach to children. And it has to do with how we integrate our short- and long-term goals for children with their own ways and needs.

If we want quality in day care we will have to deal not only with the money issues, and with the concrete issues of group size, teacher/child ratios, space, equipment, activities, and teacher qualifications, but also with the more will-o'-the-wisp aspects of child care. Do we really want to continue the present trend toward putting academic skills into programs for the youngest children? What about the place of *play* in the lives of little children as a source of delight in exploring, in learning, and in social interaction? Do we believe in its importance? If so, can we define what we want it to mean in day care? Then, what about the encouragement of each child's individuality within the institution of day care? Do we want to do that? If we do, how can it be made possible in the day-care setting? Are there other aspects of child development that should be named and underlined? What about the values that we know children acquire, even the youngest babies, from the adults who care for them? For example, should the focus of learning be on property rights of the individual or on sharing? On independence or compliance? Or on some mixture of these? Can we afford to leave this kind of difficult-to-pin-down question simply up to the discretion of individual care givers without bothering to find out what the children are actually learning in their day-to-day care away from home?

Such questions need to become part of our debate and awareness. Even if we do not all agree on what the answers should be, it is important to identify the personal and social issues, and the kinds of skills and attitudes millions of children are, or are not, acquiring long before kindergarten or first grade.

If we do not bring these questions out in the open, we are in danger of drifting into more and more rigid institutionalization of young children's lives. The purpose of this book is to focus on the questions and to increase our understanding of children's experience by holding a magnifying glass over the small daily exchanges of day care.

1 In Search of Answers

A 3-year-old sat at a table with a sheet of newspaper. First he crumpled it. Then he tried to tear it in two. When it wouldn't come apart he held it above his head and tried again. After much experimenting, he found that he could tear it if he held it with both hands and pulled with a twisting motion. Next he tore little pieces off from the edge, and on and on he worked in different ways until he had finally reduced it to a mouse's nest of scraps.

This was a film I showed to a group of day-care teachers and care givers during a workshop in Boston. As the leader, I had chosen this short film to go along with a session on curriculum. I expected the film to stimulate a discussion about the use of everyday materials, children's projects, and fine motor coordination. Instead it sparked an entirely different kind of discussion, one quite separate from anything I had planned.

The first question asked by one of the teachers was: "If you let children tear up paper like that in day care, won't they go home and tear up the books?" After a few seconds of silence everyone in the group had something to say on the subject. They talked about children's ability to discriminate between home and school, about destructive behavior versus exploration, and about control.

I found out from this session and others like it that a concrete example, a short film of children in action, makes it possible to get away from the dictatorship of experts. Each person can see and judge events for him or herself. Rather than being told what to think, individuals are thinking for themselves, and sharing their ideas. In the discussions that follow, the teacher, or leader, then becomes a more equal participant as the group tries to reach some consensus of opinion or understanding.

THROUGH THE CAMERA'S EYE

When I started using film with groups of adults I did not know how it would work. All the time that I was learning to use it as a teaching tool, I was also accumulating more and more questions. These had to do not only with learning and teaching among adults but also with questions concerning day care itself. I listened to the teachers and studied my growing collection of films. What was it really like to be a day-care teacher? And what was it like to be an infant or child in all-day group care? What happened inside those protective walls for 6, 7, or 8 hours? What was the life that the children were leading? My camera gave me a way to find some answers to these questions.

I decided to film as wide a spectrum of day care as I was able to reach, both in the United States and abroad. The decision to stick to center care and not to visit home day-care groups was principally to set some limit on so large a project. Within the centers the activities that I chose to film were free times, project times, circle times, mealtimes, nap times, and the transitions between. In addition, I tried to reach as broad a social and economic spectrum as I could in as many localities as I was able. Most of the centers that I saw were nonprofit and partially government supported, a few were private nonprofit, and some were centers run by for-profit chains. All of them were in cities or near cities.

The following is a rough breakdown of visits within the United States. On the East Coast the centers that I visited were in and around Boston. On the West Coast they were largely in various parts of Southern California, with one in Berkeley. I made one visit in Colorado. Four of these centers I was able to revisit over a number of years, several over a number of weeks, and most centers I visited more than once. In all I saw 41 centers in this country and filmed in 15 of them. In Europe the countries I visited were West Germany, Austria, Italy, Switzerland, Finland, and Sweden. I filmed in one or two centers in each of these countries but was unable to make return visits, so I did not use the material extensively.

I wanted to collect materials that I could share with others that would throw light on the processes and events of day-care days. At first I assumed that I would put these scenes into short films for teaching. Knowing that there is no more vulnerable group than the parents and teachers who deal with these earliest years of growth and development, I tried to steer clear of obvious failures to provide good care. An exposé of bad situations would not make useful teaching materials. I was looking instead for illuminating or successful exchanges between teachers and children. I wanted to record the best situations for children, and I needed to discover what these looked like in day care.

However, when I chose a center to visit, I found that I could not judge with any certainty whether I would find examples of good care. In part the wide range of communities I visited made this difficult. A first glance was not enough to understand what the best situation looked like, particularly in the cultural groups that were very different from my own. And, of course, I never knew where or when I would find a skilled teacher. Inevitably I stumbled onto some poor, even bad, moments of child care, along with all the positive ones that I saw. These negative examples were included in this book only when I felt that they made a point about child development that had to be addressed.

Having no clear ideas about what I would find, I tried to suspend judgment as much as possible while I looked. I wanted to see first and assess afterwards, and I had to learn how to do this. It was my camera lens that made this approach even thinkable. Inevitably every decision in such a project is in one sense or another a subjective one. The centers I chose, the groups in those centers, the children and the activities in those groups that I filmed, all had to be choices based on some form of judgment. But the camera allowed me both to confirm in exact detail what I thought I saw and to see what I entirely missed while I was on the spot. Often it was not until later, after reviewing a scene, that I found out what had actually happened. This made it easier to suspend judgments that might influence filming, such as turning away from a scene that appeared to be an example of poor teaching or of little importance.

CONCLUSION

From the mass of pictures that I collected, a number of related scenes began to stand out in my mind under different topics. These topics had to do with aspects of day care that eventually became the chapters of this book. In fact they became the reason for writing it. I found that I wanted to share what I had seen, as well as my conclusions, with parents and teachers in more detail than I would be able to in a class, or in a number of short films. At the same time, I wanted to put my observations in a form that was familiar to me from my teaching experience with film, one that depended heavily on specific examples. I wanted to make a kind of travel guide through a great variety of centers, picking out particular areas in the day-care lives of children that I thought needed underlining. So the book is not an overview of day care, or a How-To manual. Instead it most closely resembles a series of seminars using film, each with a separate, loosely related theme. In this way I have tried to create the same climate for independent thought as might be found in a successful group discussion.

Chapter 2 lays out the background of the day-care world and introduces my general point of view. After that, I include more and more descriptive material drawn directly from my films and site visits. Chapter 3 has to do with the abilities of young children to control themselves. Chapters 4 and 5 deal with the ways in which communication is learned in the early years. Chapter 6 points out the variety of adult values that are transmitted by interactions between teachers and children in day care. In Chapter 7 an infant-toddler teacher describes her understanding of what constitutes good care and her feelings about her work. Chapter 8 is a general discussion of *how* children learn, using Chapter 7 as a reference point. In each chapter I have freely expressed my own attitudes, interpretations, ideas, and doubts, along with related ideas of others in the field, but my hope is that readers will have enough illustrative material to come to their own conclusions about the answers that I suggest for the questions I have asked.

OTHER VOICES

The use of film or video for a more formal study of children in natural group settings is subject to some pitfalls. The picture can easily be manipulated even without conscious intent, insofar as it mirrors the movement of the human eye. Where the camera is pointed, how long a specific action is followed, and when and where in-camera cuts are made, all editorialize.

In addition, Elizabeth F. Loftus (1979) in *Eyewitness Testimony* writes about how expectations affect perception. She identifies "four different sorts of expectations that will affect perception: cultural expectations or stereotypes, expectations from past experience, personal prejudices, and momentary or temporary expectations"(p. 37). Any one of these can distort what one sees, with or without a camera. A way to correct for this would be to use a wide angle of view, with the camera in a stable position, and without cuts. Because in my own work I am not using a camera to do research in any formal sense, I film and edit more freely, picking and choosing what I think will stimulate observation, thought, and discussion.

On the positive side for all kinds of film studies is the fact that moving pictures and video can be viewed over and over again. Different individuals can view a scene. Individuals or groups from other cultures can view it. Videotapes of naturalistic scenes were used for cross-cultural studies in the recent book *Preschool in Three Cultures: Japan, China, and the United States* (Tobin, Wu, & Davidson, 1989). Still another advantage is that the same material can be reviewed over time, as understanding changes or knowledge increases.

2 The Day-Care Day

"William, are you supposed to be in the doll corner?" These words were called across the 3-year-old room by an attentive young teacher.

Every child in the room had chosen his or her own area for this "free play" period. Generally they were expected to stay with the activity they had originally chosen. Some children were gathered around the sand table. Others were at the sink. One child was at a standing easel, and some were sitting at the tables with puzzles or games. At one side of the room was a "block corner" and next to it was the "doll corner." It was a busy, varied scene.

William and Tony, both just under 3 years, were the only children using the block corner. This was a spacious area with shelves on two sides, where standard wooden building blocks were all neatly stacked, along with a few trucks, cars, and animals. There were also some small blocks, which were the ones the boys had begun playing with.

It was easy to see that William was the principal builder, while Tony hovered over him with suggestions. But soon they had used up all the little blocks and although there were enough big ones on the shelves to fill the whole area with structures, the boys apparently did not want to use them. Instead they alternated between walking around their completed building, making small adjustments to it, and going to look over a wall of plastic milk cartons into the adjoining doll corner. There, four girls were talking while setting the table. One 3-year-old girl, in particular, noticed the boys with interest.

But when William and Tony finally stepped around the wall, partly as a challenge, and uncertain of their welcome, the teacher called out to them. They were supposed to be playing with blocks.

But they wanted to play with the girls. They were drawn toward the interesting drama that seemed to be unfolding around the table. The girls, on their part, were not unreceptive, so the boys hung around between the block and doll corners, using neither, and bringing down a steady drizzle of teacher disapproval on their heads.

It was only when cleanup time came that the boys flew into purposeful and approved action. Then they put away their small heap of blocks almost with one motion, proud to be the first children in the room to be finished with cleanup.

This minidrama, which is only incidentally about the familiar boy-girl division in the nursery, illustrates a number of restrictions that erode children's confidence in themselves and hinder their creative use of the day-care environment—the exploring and experimenting and enjoying that should be the essence of learning for this age group.

As in the above example, the building blocks, which can provide children with opportunities for creative and experimental play, are often put into limited and limiting corners. In addition, teachers seldom allow materials and projects to overflow their circumscribed boundaries. The teacher could have helped William and Tony to fit their block play into the girls' tea party. The boys might have supplied blocks to be used for food, or built a pathway for the girls to follow into the block corner to visit them, or to shop, or simply to build their own structures.

Any number of scenarios might have evolved if the program rules had been less inflexible. Instead, the children were held to a predetermined plan of the kind that can make day care seem repressive and sterile, despite the hard work and dedication of the teachers. In fact, teachers themselves can become trapped in a system that does not nourish the children, and they may not see how to change it.

Everyone wants day care to be more than a warehouse to hold the children. Why then is the kind of play that encourages cognitive and social learning so often being pinched off? Several aspects of nursery life that are necessary and present in all programs may inadvertently be one cause. A close look at the ways in which space, time, routines, transitions, and curriculum are planned and managed in a number of different day-care centers suggests some very specific answers to the question of why such a gulf so often exists between practice and theory.

SPACE

One Room

The most common blueprint for day-care space is one room to one group. Although it is reassuring to children to have a special place of their own when away from home, to have that as the only place they inhabit all day can be very restricting. For some children it may mean 8 hours in that one room with brief periods outdoors if the weather is nice. This is a widely accepted way of keeping track of young children in groups, but it is not always based on necessity. I say this because I have often seen programs that do not use the available spaces that they have in order to give children a more natural environment to move around in during their long day. Out of the centers I have visited, only two directors were able to increase the opportunities for some freer movement. They did this by regularly opening up several rooms with different activities in them for the children to choose among. It is much more common, however, for day-care centers to imitate the grade-school "homeroom" model, as though there were really no basic differences between 2-year-olds and 8-year-olds. But the younger children live in their day-care rooms often for 8 hours or more, whereas the grade-school children are only in their homerooms for a part of each day.

Privacy

A child's experience in going to a day-care center has been compared to the adult experience of going to work. Some of the same stresses are in both places, the pressure to get there, the necessity to stay, the fatigue of being a public person for many hours at a time. But there is one major difference. For the children there may be no moments of privacy, even in the toilet.

This can be extremely tiring, even stressful for some children. In the home there are almost always places where a small child can withdraw for a little while, under the bed, behind a door, or alone in a room of his or her choosing. There are day-care teachers, especially those working with infant/toddler programs, who have also found various ways to supply this kind of privacy by making special spaces where a child can go to get away from the group. Perhaps because infant/toddler day care is still a comparatively new service in most of the centers that now provide it, it may be easier for the teachers to do more creative planning around the developmental needs of these youngest children.

In one room I visited, the teachers had used huge scarves to make a cave or house into which a child could creep. The scarves were thin and so the interior was light. The space had also been made inviting with a rug, pillows, and picture books.

Another infant/toddler center had two small rooms off the central area. One was empty except for a few large, cloth-covered sponge blocks. This meant, of course, that anyone able to toddle or crawl could make the decision to leave the nursery room and could be out of sight of adults and away from other children for a brief time. While I was observing, one 11-month-old went directly into the little room from his nap. When I looked in he was trying to roll a wheel-shaped block. Sometimes he fell over and sometimes it fell over. Here was a very small child playing alone, exhibiting the same relaxed concentration that he might have at home. Needless to say, older children would also benefit from this type of opportunity to be alone for some part of their time in day care.

Independence

The possibility of being apart from others now and then is a necessary element in the development of independence. At home we would worry if our children never left our sides to venture out of sight. Normally, as home-reared preschoolers get older they are encouraged to move a little farther from their principal care giver and stay away a little longer. Their growing ability to be alone and to entertain themselves is valued. Independence and responsibility for self are actively cultivated. There comes a moment when we hear the creeping baby or toddler go into the bathroom. This time we wait to follow, giving him a chance to use what he has learned and to be responsible for his own safety, even if only for a few seconds.

In many homes the door from the kitchen opens into the living room, and the door from the living room opens into the bedroom or the bathroom. For the child these are symbolic pathways into a steadily widening world.

In the day-care center the situation is dramatically reversed. Doorways become barriers that require a teacher's permission to cross, and they usually remain figuratively closed, even when the children are 4 and 5. At home the child of 4 has moved far beyond the limits set for a 1-year-old, but in day care we often see that these limits have not changed appreciably. What does that do to development?

When children are raised primarily at home their experiences generally move out month by month like the yearly rings in a tree. In day-care groups this does not happen without special planning. But even with limited space and funds, teachers and administrators who value the growth of independence and self-management skills in young children can find ways to include some of the same ingredients in day care that promote these skills in good home care. One obvious method is to make the spaces in the centers more like home spaces, with two or three interconnecting rooms. When this is not possible, other ways can be devised to enable children to follow a developmental movement outward from the cradle, with all that this means for feelings of confidence and self-esteem. For instance, children can be sent around the center on errands, and for visits, and in some cases hallways can be used imaginatively. I saw one center that had enclosed a section of well-lighted hall with low nursery gates. Down the middle was a bright stripe of color and 2-year-olds from the adjoining room could use this space at will when their door was open, taking a truck or a doll to play with.

Decision Making

Children who become accustomed to center care from an early age are not necessarily more independent than children at home. They accept being put into this larger social environment because they must, but this should not be confused with independent functioning as demonstrated by a child's own decision-making abilities.

Parents and teachers alike want children to learn how to make good decisions, but with these youngest children, teachers often think they are teaching decision making when in fact they are not offering real opportunities. If a teacher asks, "Do you want to play in the doll corner or in the block corner?" the question gives the child a clearly defined area for making a choice, but it is not the same experience for the child as making a decision where the options are not controlled by an adult. Of course, this forced choice can be a pleasant and useful experience, and it can help the teacher to manage the immediate future in a way that is comfortable for the group. Parents also use this technique.

However, on the familiar pathways of home, as children begin to move away from the primary care giver for short periods, there are many opportunities for more personal decisions. From an early age children use what they have learned about the physical environment, what they have been taught by the human environment, and their own spontaneous desires in order to make these decisions. It is therefore important to ask how much of this kind of experience can be made available in day care?

Skillful teachers are able to let children make genuine decisions within the social context that are not adult-directed. In a visit to one day-care center I watched a teacher let a 3-year-old girl remain in the doll corner during a group story time. There were reasons why this particular child preferred to go on playing with a doll. She was new at the center, and she spoke very little English, so the closeness to other children and the questions often asked in group time may have felt threatening to her. In any case this teacher let her know that she was not forgotten, without any overtones of disapproval. The child had made a genuine decision to stay away from the group, which her teacher respected.

In a different center I watched a parallel situation, again with a 3-year-old girl. This child, although strongly urged, refused to go and sit with the group. She also had a language problem. But instead of having her decision respected, it was treated as bad behavior. So when she tried to help an assistant who was preparing materials for a table project, the assistant stopped her. "You can't have fun helping me when you're not going to group."

This last story shows how easy it is to slip from limited space into limited options. If there is only one room, it readily turns into emphasis on one activity; everyone eat, everyone sleep, everyone clean up, line up, or sit in a circle together. Such a program may give an appearance of pleasant orderliness to the visitor, but limited space can turn all too easily into limited learning under a regime of too much order.

TIME

Time is another important factor in the lives of day-care children. It may actually be the key factor in making the day-care environment a productive, happy place. But when center days are divided into inflexible time periods, the schedules are placing tight restrictions on children's meaningful activities just at a period in their lives when some freedom to reach out on their own is central to learning.

Necessities

Practical necessities are at least a partial explanation for this scheduling. The 8-hour day, instead of giving teachers a sense of more time, seems to give less. The teacher, or teachers, no matter how many they are, have an enormous number of activities to plan and get through. Children in center care need to be fed at least three times, sometimes four, with snacks or meals. In addition to feeding them the teachers have to see that the children get washed, have time for the toilet, for going outside, for rest. Then there is the problem of keeping the physical environment in some order. Teachers with 15 or more preschool children in one room for 8 hours have to have some method of controlling objects, the furniture, toys, and materials of nursery school. Also, the teacher in charge is expected and expects herself or himself to provide a visible curriculum. And finally, of course, there are the teachers' own personal needs for time out.

Saving Free Time

Clearly an organized system is necessary to deal with all these practicalities. But the system should serve the children and their teachers, not the reverse. Too much emphasis on organization is counterproductive. There needs to be an emphasis on saving as much constructive free time as possible for children out of the organized 8-hour day. By free time I mean time free of adult pressures, time for teacher attention that is nondirective, time for children to practice self-management and to play in different social patterns. Children need time to play alone if they wish, as well as with others, time to explore and experiment with materials, and time for make-believe. When a teacher knows how to support the children's own projects, free time becomes the curriculum time. In addition it can serve as a partial substitute for more varied space. But in many centers where this valuable free time is absent, rigid transitions and routines are often the cause.

TRANSITIONS AND ROUTINES

Transitions can be "wild" times, as one director described them to me, where children move about, stretch, and joke as they get ready for the next activity, like a flock of birds who fly up in disarray and then settle back into their tree. They also can become burdensome periods of waiting for the last coat to be buttoned, or total silence to descend. Yet preschool children are not good at doing nothing. For some of the very young to sit still and wait is a near physiological impossibility, and this is not really "cured" by pressure and practice but only by growth and development. Teachers who spend their energies trying to get preschool children to be silent and immobile are misusing their own time as well as the children's. If the children cannot comply, teachers and children alike feel unsuccessful. If the children do learn to stay still during long waiting periods, that may mean that they are learning passivity, and children who are taught to be passive and blindly obedient cannot be expected to become self-motivated, self-managing individuals.

Of course, different day-care programs have different organizational styles depending on cultural, physical, and personal factors. There is no one right way to manage, any more than there is one right way to run a household.

Preparing for Lunch

The three examples below show the various ways in which routines and transitions save time or waste it. The groups were closely matched in size and in the ages of the children. Each group was about 17 in number; all were groups of 3-year-olds; all had no more than one room per group.

In the first center the room was on the small side, but it seemed even smaller because almost every inch that was not taken up by the long lunch table was filled with cots. The children were waiting for the food to be delivered from the kitchen. The teacher was frustrated and angry because she was unable to keep one little boy on his bed. In this transition time between the end of the morning and lunch the cots had been put down and each child was supposed to stay quietly, without talking, on his or her bed until lunch was on the table. The children could hardly grasp this apparently irrational plan. One child got out a puzzle and sat at the table to work. She was quickly restored to her bed, without the puzzle. Another child whose cot was next to the bookcase started to pull out books for himself and a friend. He was made to put them back. These were unintentional infractions, but the child that the teacher was most upset with was dodging away from her among the beds.

Quite aside from the negative learning involved, all this attempt to keep the children inactive was a waste of time. The teacher had designed a way of managing the lunch routines that held the children in limbo during a transition and made her own role nearly impossible. If you transferred this plan to a home, it would quickly become apparent that to make a child go to bed before lunch in order to be out of the way, and then afterwards to rest again, would not be pleasant or sensible.

In the second center, there was the same system of putting the cots down before lunch, but the scene was very different. Although the children were supposed to sit on their cots until lunch was ready, they were encouraged to sit with a friend. Talk and books were allowed, which meant a good deal of coming and going to and from the bookshelves. It was a warm, sociable, relaxed time in which the children could also make reassuring contact with their teacher, showing her pictures and asking questions while she worked at the lunch wagon. Their time was not being wasted.

My third observation was in a room where the morning's activities flowed more directly into lunchtime, and where the cots were put down after the meal. Here all the children were not doing the same thing during the transition. While some helped to set out the cups and napkins, others were still putting away their toys, still others washing their hands. One boy remained engrossed in a drawing that he was doing at the table. The student teacher was pressing him to stop, without success. When the head teacher came over, her solution to the situation was to set the table around him, thus giving him a few more minutes to come to a stopping place.

The way of breaking up the activities in this center, so that the children were not all going through the transition from the morning activities to mealtime in lockstep, or waiting idly, became a partial substitute for a more homelike, flexible space. The teacher's technique of orchestrating rather than ordering made it possible for time to be flexible, which in turn made room for individualized responses to the children, as with the boy absorbed in his drawing.

Judging Development

Routines and transitions that involve eating, getting dressed to go outside when the weather is cold, putting away toys, brushing teeth, and going to the toilet all entail specific behaviors and physical skills that young children are learning to master in their first years, whether at home or in day care. At home they are often a source of conflict. By comparison the children in day care seem to pick them up more easily, probably because of reinforcement from the group. They imitate each other and do not feel singled out by what may seem to them a parent's irrational demands. This can be one of the aspects of group care that is positive for young children.

However, some teachers push too hard for standards that are too rigorous. They apparently do not realize how well the children are doing, and feel responsible for teaching these daily living skills. They misjudge developmental levels, actually setting standards of behavior more stringent than even school-age children are expected to meet. When this happens, when routines are handled without regard for their real purpose, this can spoil the pleasure of eating, take the satisfaction out of achievement, and inhibit the positive ways in which children use materials and toys. For instance, I have seen a silent 4-year-old group eating in semidarkness as a punishment. Whatever the pressures on this teacher, she was distorting the normal flow of life in her day-care room in order to try to produce required behavior in the children. Later when talking to the director I asked her about this, and she said it was a solution definitely against their policy. Presumably she helped her teacher find another way to teach desired behavior.

Getting Dressed

In another setting I watched a group of 3-year-olds get ready to go out on a cold day. Their teacher, before leaving the room, told them to get dressed and line up. With a little help from the assistant they all got themselves into hats, heavy jackets, and some even put on their mittens. Once ready and lined up by the door, they had to wait a few minutes for their teacher. There was some giggling, pushing, and teasing but no fights or tears or running around the room.

When the teacher returned, however, instead of praising them for their real achievement in getting dressed, she scolded them for not being quiet. Then she made them sit in a circle as punishment, where she told them that they were wasting their own outdoor time. Later I saw her through the window enjoying the outdoor play period with her group, she herself running and laughing. She was a warm, responsive teacher, but apparently she had felt it was her job to enforce this standard of social behavior, and she had not given the children sufficient help to meet her standard or questioned whether it was reasonable.

Cleanup

Cleanup time is another routine that deserves special attention, because it has become elevated out of all proportion to the rest of the day. Too often cleanup periods become an end in themselves, accompanied by admonitions and criticisms. "Teach the children to pick up their toys" has traveled out of the How-To child-rearing books into day-care programs like a powerful echo, with more moral than practical overtones. Block play is one common casualty. William and his friend are an example of children who learn how to avoid the stress of these cleanup times. They used only the smallest blocks to make the smallest possible structure.

An observation in a different 3-year-old room suggests how children get to be so restricted in their block play. This room had the blocks in a kind of stall between two shelves. Although it was cramped, it also had a potential advantage. Block structures could be left up for the day, or even overnight, because the space was not used for any other purpose. Several boys were in this space during the free-play time. They pulled blocks and boards and small toys into a heap on the floor. Then they spent the rest of the period negotiating for cars or running them along the blocks in a random fashion. They built nothing, appeared bored, and clearly needed encouragement to use these blocks. In this case the teacher didn't get to them until cleanup time, when she literally scolded the blocks back onto the shelves, as though she were using the children as a broom. One could only suppose, because cleaning up was so unpleasant, that next time these children would do even less. She too was actually a good teacher in other ways, but she seemed to feel that there was something so special about cleanup that she suspended all her usual warmth and teaching skills during the dread ritual.

For many centers this episode summarizes the problem. Teachers are under pressure to get from one part of the program to the next, but some increase this pressure by measuring their success by how quiet, orderly, and obedient the children are during these times. From my own observations this kind of standard directs focus away from enhancing children's play to seeing that they clean up at the end of it. In the block corners, because buildings are seldom allowed to stay up, children respond by hardly using the blocks at all. Along with learning to put away their toys, children may finally learn not to take them out. For example, William and Tony with their minibuilding had made a real decision of the type I have discussed when they chose not to build a large, ambitious structure. It was a good decision for their day, but a bad decision for their future.

CURRICULUM

It is difficult to prescribe standards for programming the daily activities of children, not only because of the cultural differences between communities but also because there is a double message in the air. On the one hand, parents and day-care teachers want preschool children to be preparing for future academic success. This objective, however, tends to be interpreted, or misinterpreted, as requiring earlier and earlier teaching of the symbols and the social behaviors deemed necessary for grade school. On the other hand, child development literature designed to guide parents and teachers stresses the need for young children to be encouraged to use their muscles, to use their senses, to develop their imaginations, make decisions, and think for themselves. These important experiences for children's development don't have to be in conflict with preparation for the school years ahead, but at present they often are. As a result some centers unwittingly let their programs fall into the rigid patterns that do not promote learning, even as they try to fulfill all the requirements for excellence.

Many conscientious day-care teachers think that curriculum specifically means activities that are prescribed as well as supervised by them, usually with a readily visible result. If a child learns the days of the week, has a picture to take home, and can do a puzzle, these are visible results. And of course there do need to be some of these results for the pleasurable sharing of accomplishments between parents, teachers, and children. Also, some direct introduction to cultural symbols, days and clocks, pictures and letters, is certainly valuable. But a curriculum is not of much value to children when it is seen as taking place almost entirely during table projects, or while children are sitting all together in a floor circle with a teacher who simply asks them questions and gives out disconnected kinds of information.

Table Projects

Tightly organized table projects are, in fact, a staple in most day-care rooms. This is part of a curriculum emphasis on small muscle skills, visual skills, and language. These are important areas of learning and this is one way in which to learn. However, because of the length of time spent at table activities, the lack of variation from day to day, and the prescriptive nature of the projects, some centers seem to have lost sight of the larger purpose and are simply intent on keeping children quietly occupied. Many different projects can be fun, and at first interesting, but when children move in a routine way from doing a puzzle, to outlining shapes with a magic marker, to Play-Doh, to a lotto game, and when this is the same fare every day, it is a sterile diet. It restricts learning by its very meagerness as well as its consumption of time.

As an alternative, a rich curriculum of information and skills can be incorporated into the freer play of children. Although teachers are not always good at inventing new ways of using familiar materials, children usually are if given an opportunity. One easy way to break out of this mediocrity of experience is to watch for the children's own ideas. When teachers support the ideas of children rather than squelching them as unorthodox, they find their programs becoming more varied, with the children more animated and enjoying.

Those teachers who expect to get ideas from children, instead of always expecting themselves to be giving, can then find ways to add to and enrich the play. For example, one day I saw a 4-year-old child decide to stick Play-Doh on a painting he was doing at the table. The teacher noticed that this looked like a relief map, so she suggested that the dough could be mountains or islands. When the child responded with enthusiasm, the teacher handed him a small boat to run between the lumps. Other children liked this idea and started to try it too. Because this teacher welcomed a different way of using the materials, later that morning mountains and rivers appeared in the sand table. Even though this is how concepts are formed, teachers seldom get the same enthusiastic feedback from other teachers and from parents that they get for teaching children to memorize numbers or the days of the week. Consequently many tend to feel more successful when they are passing on information directly in a formal teaching session than when they are helping children to learn through their own creative activities the concepts and insights that represent more internal growth.

Circle Times

Once I saw a teacher who had been trained in China keep a group of 15 four-year-olds absolutely fascinated for over an hour. Young children's attention can be held in highly structured situations when there is enough opportunity to move, enough surprise and suspense, a frequent change of pace, and the involvement of every child either as observer or performer. Here the teacher had the children getting up and down, clapping, singing, reciting in unison, going to the center to perform by twos and threes, and on and on with variations. But this represented training from another culture, one with presumably different goals from ours. Few teachers in the United States have this kind of expert training.

For us, all too often, with our trend toward earlier introduction of academics, circle times are getting longer and longer and—as a consequence—dull and oppressive for the children. The results are poor. Sitting together in a group for short periods can be a positive experience for young children, but not when timing and expectations of specific behaviors run directly counter to important developmental tasks, like being able to learn by listening. Thirty or forty minutes in a circle—which I have seen more than once—is too long for most preschool children to sit still in a group while staying focused on a teacher. Instead of listening, many must concentrate on being quiet and immobile.

In one 3-year-old room, I saw a teacher who had style and flexibility at other times, but who became frozen into one repeated format during these group sessions. She had the children sitting for 45 minutes while she tried to teach them the days of the week, the months, colors, numbers, and shapes. When she finally got out a picture book, it was not to read the children a story but to teach them the names of different breeds of dog. Her only technique was to ask questions, then supply the answer, then ask again. Every few minutes she had to stop and scold someone for moving out of place, talking to a neighbor, or "not paying attention." In the end four boys, who had been perfectly respectful, found it impossible to rise to her expectations. They kept whispering and wiggling, so were punished by being made to sit still even longer after the other children were released. In this situation the teacher's effort was 100%, whereas her success was almost zero. After the first few minutes none of the children could answer her questions.

Another 3-year-old group had a teacher who was particularly good at responding immediately to any child as she moved through the morning. Her strength lay in her ability to give individual attention to the children. She gave information, suggestions, and support during the free time, demonstrating how preschool children can acquire knowledge without being vigorously restricted in order for learning to take place. But circle time defeated her. First she sang a verse of "Old McDonald." Some of the children sang along with her. However, when she asked them to volunteer the name of an animal to sing about in the next verse, the children were completely at a loss. They had just sung about a chicken, so one child volunteered "chicken." Because no further suggestions were forthcoming, the teacher started calling on individual children. One child mumbled a word that the teacher could not understand, another said "baseball," another said "red," and, picking up on this, still another child said "Like that," pointing to a red stop sign. On a shelf behind these children were a number of rubber animals that could easily have been passed around, but they were ignored. In the circle-time format their teacher had totally abandoned what she really knew, that children learn by touching, seeing, and doing, just as the first teacher had forgotten that children with their immature nervous systems often learn best when they are allowed to move.

CONCLUSION

These current structures of day-care days, along with the emphasis on formal teaching and on conformity, can mean that even centers with the most careful plans may end up actually minimizing what the children learn. It is indeed important for children to learn to sit still or clean up or recite the days of the week. But it is far more important for them to learn that they can learn, both through their own efforts and from their teachers, and that it is rewarding and pleasurable to do so. This is the single most important preacademic lesson of the preschool years. It is cause for concern when children instead are taught that learning from adults is unpleasant, or that they are unable to learn what the adult world values. When young children are pressured to get ready for the future with negatives and sterile exercises, and in ways that run counter to development, then the results can be far more crippling than a late academic start.

OTHER VOICES

When day care becomes rigidly institutionalized it can actually create problem children. Often these are the gifted, the energetic, or the self-motivated.

Valerie Polakow Suransky (1982) in *The Erosion of Childhood* made a study of five day-care centers in the Midwest. She writes that in several of the centers, "children are socialized into institutional time, where time is no longer a field of presence, an abode, but an austere system of constraints demanding submission" (p. 175). And she notes that the children who were considered deviant were those who were "temporal or spatial norm violators. . . . The spontaneous, moving, energetic, playing being of the child presented a threat to these organizational structures and hence needed to be contained" (p. 176).

In *Beyond Boredom and Anxiety,* Mihaly Csikszentmihalyi (1982) describes what happens when children are not reined in too tightly or prevented from following their own interests by heavily restricted time and space. He defines, or redefines, what causes activities to be completely absorbing. Although his examples are drawn from adult experience, he believes the same principles also have application for children. Here, for example, is his definition of play.

> Anyone who stops to watch children at play will see how intrinsically rewarding action can be. What children do is "play" only by the conventional wisdom of adult perspective. One could say just as well that what they do is work. But both labels are confusing: what children do most of the time is interact with the environment on a level at which their skills match opportunities. Left to themselves, children seek out "flow" with the inevitability of natural law. They act without interruption if they can use their bodies, their hands, or their brain to produce feedback which proves that they can control the environment. They stop only when challenges are exhausted, or when their skills are. (p. 199)

Complementary to this definition of play—one of the important ways in which children learn—are T. Berry Brazelton's (1983) descriptions of the individual styles present in each infant at birth. His book *Infants and Mothers: Differences in Development,* in describing the reciprocal learning between mothers and infants, makes the point that babies and young children are not simply blank pages to be written on by concerned adults, or empty vessels to be filled. He says about the three kinds of babies he describes, "In each of these

infants, I have attempted to demonstrate the strong, inborn differences that predetermine their particular styles of development. In
each case, certain reactions from the environment are more 'appro-
priate' than others—that is, each infant can respond more easily to
parenting that fits into his capacity to receive and respond" (p.
287). Furthermore, "These babies show a resistance to being
pushed into habits that are not sympathetic to their style, a resistance backed up by all the strength inherent in any well-organized
personality, infant or adult" (p. 288). He goes on to say, "I should
like to stress again the balance between personality and cognitive
development that may be crucial to the ultimate formation of
healthy adults. When a child is 'ready' to learn a new step, he needs
little help to achieve it. When he must learn it via mechanisms that
are not yet ready, he will spend energies that may be expensively
drained from more important areas of his total development" (p.
288).

3 Self-Control
Rhythm, Repetition, and Imitation

Adult concern about control is another reason why some day-care programs become overly regimented. Control in the day-care setting can be of serious concern to teachers, just as it is to parents, who want to be sure their child is not going to be overwhelmed by the group or allowed to run wild. The most successful teachers have learned how to maintain order easily without using awkward and time-consuming techniques such as a constant emphasis on rules. They can do this because they understand that all of the controls do not have to be imposed on the children from the outside.

Children will be effective partners if allowed to build up their own spontaneous methods of self-control. In fact, children have from infancy some behaviors that can lead directly into later social skills. For example, in one infant/toddler room I saw a 10-month-old child who was on the floor turning over a large tub of plastic beads, the kind that can be fitted together or pulled apart. Other creepers were attracted to the colorful scattering of beads and came over to look and touch. When one child began to drop and throw the beads back into the tub, the rest of them, with their 1-year-old interest in putting things in and out of containers, tried to imitate him, and most succeeded. Here they were all being active in concert without conflict. When these kinds of impulses and plans are respected, then behaviors that may be accidental at first can create surprisingly orderly social situations in the group care of even these youngest children.

Children love patterned behavior. Research, particularly with mother and baby pairs, has documented how young infants respond to rhythm and repetition and how they imitate adult behaviors. I am going to pick up where these studies leave off, showing specific examples of children under 5 using these behaviors among their peers. These particular behaviors are the ones that appear in the earliest human social exchanges and are readily observable in most infant/toddler groups.

In one center I watched a 13-month-old child entertained by a shouting match with a 2-year-old on the other side of a low room divider. He saw the 2-year-old looking down at him from a small platform and called out, "Ya, ya, ya." The older child replied, "Ya, ya, ya," and the call went back and forth for almost a minute with both children intensely responding one to the other. This elementary base of communication and response is common in programs where the teachers don't view it as troublesome.

Children's early experiments in using their spontaneous behaviors in social contacts gradually lead to other behaviors, such as follow-the-leader, taking turns, sharing, and cooperation. These seem to evolve along a developmental line.

Two-year-olds when they become three-year-olds, and when they have been helped to use these spontaneous behaviors constructively during their first years, can now use them quite reliably without teacher aid. They are the tools for safe and enjoyable socializing. Follow-the-leader patterns begin to lead more consciously into taking turns. This enables children to share spaces. Then once they have learned to be together without getting into conflicts that they can't control, cooperative projects are possible.

By the time most children reach the age of 4, their practice of advanced skills like cooperation can readily be seen in the less supervised parts of their days. Sustained dramatic play is one example, with children agreeing to take different parts, someone being the father, someone the mother, and someone else the baby. Block play with elaborate houses and towers is another activity where cooperation with division of roles becomes a deliberately practiced behavior.

I don't mean to suggest that young children are naturally filled with social virtues. What I am suggesting is that they have some of their own methods for developing social skills. Teachers who provide all-day care can either reject these methods or help children have the experience of self-management. If allowed to practice their own techniques whenever possible, the children gain from feelings of competence and self-control. When this happens, it is one of the important positives of group child care, for these experiences balance what children may lose by not having a longer time for learning in the greater intimacy of home.

Yet after saying this, I want to emphasize that it is not precocious mastery of social skills that I think is of special value. There is no intrinsic benefit to be had by leaping from the cradle into a group. It is the process by which these early skills for group living are acquired that can really make the day-care experience a nourishing one for a preschool child.

ONE-YEAR-OLDS

Banging on the Lunch Table

In an infant/toddler center, I once filmed a group of six children between the ages of 10 and 14 months who were waiting for their lunch. They were sitting in low cube-chairs at a round wooden table while their teacher stood a few feet away preparing the food. First one child started to slap her hands up and down on the table top. Then the others joined her until all six were banging in approximate unison.

One-year-olds, of course, come naturally to this kind of up-and-down movement. Controlled vertical arm movements are a recently mastered gesture that they seem to enjoy enormously and almost cannot help exercising if given a stick or a spoon. In addition, their use of imitation is now a more conscious behavior than during their first months. It is also a behavior that is easily observed.

On this particular day these three aspects of early development—rhythm, repetition, and imitation—came together to create an exciting social experience for the children, a drumming session that seemed rather like a group sing. It was an experience in patterned social activity that they had invented themselves. Some smiled and they all watched each other with complete concentration as they banged.

The teacher, who was about to hand out dishes of yogurt and fruit, might well have stopped the banging, fearing that when she gave the children spoons that they would bang these too. And of course they did bang their spoons in between trying to scoop up fruit and yogurt. She asked them not to bang on the table any more, and showed them how to use their spoons for eating. Nevertheless, she understood that they could comply only intermittently, so she didn't make an issue of their failure to stop entirely. Instead she demonstrated that eating was the main activity by eating herself, and helping a child here and there to get a spoonful. She worked to guide the children with positives rather than negatives, not trying to run directly counter to the developmental skills that they were enjoying.

Teacher Rhythm and Repetition

In this case, the teacher then went on to use the children's response to rhythm and repetition in order to create another pleasing social situation at the lunch table. After they had eaten most of their yogurt, she passed around a plate of small sandwiches, helping each child with a repetitious chant. She was teaching them to take just one off the plate at a time instead of grasping for several. Her chant was, "One for you, and one for you, and one for you," with the same rising inflection for each child until she came to the last, when she dropped her voice and spoke the child's name in a kind of grand finale. The sense of order and predictability she created in this way appeared to be extremely satisfying to the children, as well as making it easy for them to wait for a turn. I noticed when I looked at my film later that one child even gave her head a little punctuating nod after the final beat.

So here is an example of children discovering a social technique and their teacher building on it. Later this same group of 1-year-olds all climbed into a play pen that had a sagging side. They then started to climb out, sometimes stepping on each other in the process. Another teacher in the room, who was sitting with an infant some yards away and watching the 1-year-olds, started a rhythmic verbal accompaniment to each child's successful descent. She said, "Get dooooown" with a dying fall inflection. This reenforced what the children were doing, which was in fact taking turns. They picked up the rhythm. Some said the word *Dooown,* and they continued to climb in and out without conflict, being reassured rather than either instructed or restricted by the teacher.

Beneath the surface of these events are many issues having to do with development, teaching techniques, social learning, and cultural goals. This is true of all the examples that I give of the spontaneous, organizing behaviors of preschool children that emerge in group situations. They raise many related questions, such as whether the 1-year-olds in this example were being taught "pack behavior" as opposed to independent functioning. However, I am passing over all the other issues in this particular discussion in order to emphasize the point that children, even under a year old, have these important potential social skills, generated by rhythm and repetition, within their own processes of development.

TWO-YEAR-OLDS

Imitation

Imitation begins to show up even more frequently among older toddlers. This can lead them into learning satisfying ways of interacting with each other. For example, a young 2-year-old found a sponge Frisbee lying in the playground of his day-care center. He had probably watched older people throwing them, because he grabbed it and gave it a toss, using his whole body with great drama. Another 2-year-old saw this grand gesture and ran after the Frisbee, picked it up, and hurled it with the same stylish enthusiasm. No doubt it was partly luck that sent the Frisbee far enough so that another child could pick it up before the first thrower arrived. Nevertheless, these two children found themselves taking turns for a couple of minutes in a way that was highly pleasurable to them both.

Follow-the-Leader

As children reach the age of 2, the kinds of follow-the-leader behavior described in the playpen episode become more conscious. Follow-the-leader serves as a social stimulus as well as an organizing tool for children who might otherwise either get into conflict or avoid each other. One day I saw several 2-year-olds in a Montessori program march repeatedly around and between two long parallel bars on a playground, one following the other. I had noticed on previous visits that many of the children in this group interacted very little with their peers. It was a program whose focus was on learning about the physical world rather than the human one. But in the procession, although the children did not speak or even seem to look at one another, they had effectively designed a social event for themselves, a parade.

Taking Turns

Often we are told that children are selfish and need to be taught to take turns. It is true, of course, that young children are self-centered and naturally so. However, this does not mean that taking turns is something that can be learned only if imposed by the adult world. Put very simplistically, imitation leads naturally into follow-the-leader behavior, and follow-the-leader behavior makes experience in taking turns almost inevitable.

Here is an example. A 4-year-old, a 3-year-old, and a 2-year-old formed a small parade across their playground until they came to a low rock. The largest child climbed over first, followed by the next largest, followed by the 2-year-old. The leader was ready to climb again before the last child in the line had gotten started. But since they had been in a clear follow-the-leader pattern, the leader waited for his follower to get over the rock; otherwise he would no longer have been a leader. If he pushed the younger children away he would have had no followers. As a 4-year-old he had become aware of patterned game behavior and how it works. Although the older children soon ran off, bored by waiting for the slower 2-year-old, the structure of their game had led them into taking turns. One can see examples of this necessary connection between following behaviors and turn-taking all the time in playgrounds, where pre-school children are apt to be most free from adult direction. As the children get older the structures become more formalized, moving from the most primitive forms of imitative behavior into elaborate games.

THREE-YEAR-OLDS

Chasing

Follow-the-leader behavior is not always intertwined with turn-taking. At one center I watched a group of 3-year-olds being led outside to play in an open space between a parking lot and a housing development. There were no fences to keep them in the safe area and there was no equipment for them to play with, but there were paths that formed a long rectangle. A couple of the children began to run and all the rest followed after. Again like a flight of birds, they all ran in one direction, then looped back with small, individual variations. They were creating a follow-the-leader pattern that contained them in a limited space while it allowed for maximum activity, along with freedom from adult interference. The children who dropped out to rest could rejoin. The most active could go as fast as they were able for as long as they wished without colliding or running among the cars. In the meantime, the teachers were watchful but relaxed. They understood the constraints that the follow-the-leader pattern put on the children, constraints that made it easy to stay in the prescribed space. This was a case of teachers and children synchronizing with each other, both understanding this spontaneous behavior and how it worked.

Two-year-olds, even one-year-olds, will respond to the fun and contagion of a group run for short periods of time or short distances. But they would not have the committed response to the patterned behavior that made these 3-year-old children feel free and in control.

Making Cupcakes

The next vignette is more complex. In this scene rhythm, repetition, and imitation all facilitate taking turns, sharing, and cooperation. Here is an example of a teacher allowing children to use their own mechanisms for self-control. This teacher was particularly fascinating to watch because of her sensitivity to these self-organizing child behaviors. On the morning that I visited she was making cupcakes with 8 of the 3-year-olds in her group of 14. The rest of the children were doing another project with an assistant, but her group stood or sat around an oblong table, where she started the project by saying, "Who has the eggs?" The materials spread out on the table consisted of a large bowl, half a carton of eggs, water, measuring cup, cake mix, a spoon for stirring, paper liners, and a large cupcake pan. The pan was lying between two of the girls who each gripped a side. They frowned and did not look at each other.

Their teacher, without saying anything, reached across the table to hand out colored paper liners for the cupcake pan, alternating, first on one side for one girl, then on the other side for the other girl. She repeated this only a couple of times before leaving the package of liners to the children, but the rhythm was clear. The children let go of the pan and concentrated on putting the liners into it until every hole was filled. At the end they touched their work gently and smiled at each other. The pattern that the teacher had set up to enable the children to relax and to share was not unlike that used by the 1-year-olds' teacher in passing the sandwiches. However, it was briefer because the children did not need continued repetition to know that there would be enough space in the pan and enough paper liners for each of them.

As this cupcake-making session continued, it was now the teacher's nonintervention that helped the children. Each child was given a chance to put some of the ingredients into the bowl as it passed slowly around the table, so there was considerable waiting time. The children who had gone first and put in the dry mix began to get restless. They started a make-believe eating game. First one child leaned way over a tin try that lay on the table and pretended to feed himself with exaggerated, repeated scoops of both hands. The girl across from him then grabbed the empty cake mix bag and shook it wildly over the tray, with a high, excited giggle. She too began to pretend to eat with fast, rhythmic gestures and she added loud accompanying grunts. For a few seconds the children were active and noisy. Then the excitement all subsided as they turned their attention to the approaching bowl that held the finished batter. The teacher, who apparently understood just what was going on, did not intervene by even a glance. When the bowl finally arrived and it was their turn for a taste, each of the mock eaters had come back to reality and was in perfect control.

This teacher clearly knew how to work with the children's responsiveness to rhythm and repetition. When the two girls were in conflict over the pan, she was able to show them how to share by using rhythm. When the restless children were managing to take care of themselves with active, noisy, rhythmic behavior, she had the perception to leave them alone to have the good experience of having controlled themselves. In fact, this seemed to be one of the purposes of the project, to teach the children that they could be in charge of themselves and she could be their guide. From the start it had been her message as she looked around the lively group of 3-year-olds and asked them for the eggs.

Follow-the-Leader Chase

The way in which this particular teacher handled transitions in between activities is also worth describing. Between the end of the cooking project and going outside, three boys who had finished their part of the cleanup started wrestling on the floor. It quickly became too rough for two of them, and it looked as though one of them was going to cry. The third child, who was the least embroiled, then jumped up and challenged the others to chase him. With an alacrity that showed what a welcome and familiar idea this was, the other boys joined him in a follow-the-leader chase around a low toy shelf. The entire episode took only seconds, but it demonstrates the way in which 3-year-olds can use follow-the-leader behavior as a tool to control unpleasant social situations that arise in their play. The chase, which is basically an organized activity, was then easily transformed into line-up behavior when the teacher told them it was time to go out, which she did promptly without saying anything about not running in the classroom.

I realize that in this instance the teacher's noninvolvement is somewhat controversial because people have different ideas of order and control. A visiting parent might well have seen her behavior as a form of neglect. The teacher, on the other hand, apparently knew these children so well and understood their patterns of self-control so completely that she decided to let them use these crude, new, social tools in the nursery room without interference. In a way, this social problem solving was hard work for 3-year-old boys. Some parents and teachers will think it was too hard, although such behavior often occurs unnoticed in playgrounds. Others may feel that the wrestling and running were breaking a code of indoor behavior that set a bad precedent.

However, this social problem-solving experience is an example of the special opportunities available to children in day-care settings. If they must be in groups for most of their waking hours, then I believe that they should be allowed to learn the necessary social skills in ways that develop ego strengths whenever possible. The teacher's priority in this situation was not maintaining her own direct control—although I expect she would have quickly intervened if needed—but rather encouraging the solution that would give the children the greatest feeling of self-control.

These trouble spots and moments of social exuberance often yield a great deal of information about a teacher as well as about the program's general approach to child care. Noninterference is not always a good way of teaching, but generally speaking, the scolding and negative reenforcement that are so often used to maintain control do not teach much to preschool children besides avoidance. Children are capable of learning much more.

Mob Rule

Because the 3-year-old year is one of enormous social growth, it is also a time of some rather extreme experimentation. And sometimes these experiments demonstrate the negative possibilities in children's attraction to rhythm, repetition, and imitation. In one 3-year-old group that I visited, the teacher started the transition from morning to lunchtime with a repeated sing-song announcement, "Time to clean up . . . time to clean up . . . ." In this instance, however, instead of soothing the children and helping them to wind down their play, the rhythm had the opposite effect. They imitated the teacher's sing-song and under the leadership of one inspired girl, the chant quickly escalated into a screaming match with every child making as much noise as possible. The leader screamed so hard that her face turned purple. It took only a few seconds for the drama to reach this point. Then the teacher put her hands over her ears and said at a normal voice level, "That hurts my ears." She did this three times, which was all the support the children needed to stop a behavior that had apparently begun to feel unpleasantly out of control even for them. As an observer I got the feeling that they themselves didn't like what had happened, because of the serious expressions on their faces at the end and the speed with which they quieted down and started to put away their toys.

In this difficult situation, when the children were all screaming, the teacher was able to turn it to their advantage. Here I think the absence of a negative response from the teacher kept the unpleasantness from continuing and enabled the children to concentrate on the event itself. Or put in another way, the teacher did not distract them from the disagreeable experience by taking up their attention with a scolding. Perhaps the preschool years may be our best opportunity to let children find out what these powerful natural impulses feel like when they have gone awry. Teachers can help children learn when to be enjoying members of a group, and when to turn away from propulsive activities that turn into group hysteria and mob rule. However, they themselves need to understand the developmental processes involved in such behaviors.

CONCLUSION

To the outsider, this business of developing self-control can sometimes look like its opposite, messy and uncontrolled behavior. But teachers who let the process unfold are actually providing programs that recognize the positive nature of children. These are programs that are not based solely on adult assumptions and the patterns of adult behavior. Young children's timing is different from that of adults, faster in some things and slower in others. Likewise, the self-controlling behaviors of preschool children are not usually ones that adults prescribe, as in the case of the chasing games. Child-designed social skills tend to be more active than circumspect. The children in the cooking class were not being quiet or sitting still while they were practicing self-control.

A question that may reasonably be asked is how children are going to learn school-age behavior if their teachers don't immediately stop them when they behave in ways that would be unacceptable in older children. Part of the answer is that physical maturation itself modifies these early behaviors. At the same time the children's understanding of the social milieu and of their culture is constantly growing. Acted-out social skills become increasingly internalized as time passes. Even so, for some years those behaviors that adults impose in order to control excited children are not the ones that children use themselves. Although children may sometimes welcome being told to sit down and be quiet, this is not a control that they can depend on when no teacher is near.

Day-care children who are able to experience at an early age self-control that is not based on fear of their teacher's displeasure will have a more positive sense of themselves than children who are constantly told, in effect, "Don't do it your way. Do it my way. Your way is wrong." Teachers will have more time. Children will have more confidence that they can successfully meet adult expectations. In short, the ways in which preschool teachers teach social skills and handle the issues of control surely matter a great deal for the children's long-run development. It is not just what is taught, but also how that is important.

OTHER VOICES

Infant studies make it clear why children in the next stages of development are responsive to rhythm as well as to the repetitions and imitation that play so prominent a role in their first social experiences.

Daniel Stern (1977) in *The First Relationship: Infant and Mother* is looking at the meaning of synchrony among humans, in this case specifically between babies and their mothers. He describes his research, and his conclusions about timing and repetition and imitation in mother/baby communications. "It appears that virtually all complex social human activities, including most interpersonal exchanges, require the simultaneous consideration of programmed behavioral sequences and of the stimulus-response paradigm" (p. 89).

His later book, *The Diary of a Baby* (1990), is full of concrete examples of these interactions, along with his more fanciful interpretations. For instance, Stern describes a mother's response to her crying 6-week-old infant.

Like many mothers faced with a hungry, crying baby, she keeps on talking to him, sometimes nonstop, until the nipple is securely in his mouth. . . . She also uses her voice as a pacemaker, at first going faster than the beat of Joey's cries, to override his rhythm; then she slows to bring him down with her to a less excited state. (p.37)

The anthropologist Edward T. Hall (1977) is interested from another perspective in the cultural differences and biological similarities in the way people use their bodies, as well as in differences in concepts of time and space. In his book *Beyond Culture,* there is a particularly relevant chapter called "Rhythm and Body Movement," in which he gives examples of children's play behavior as part of his more general discussion. After describing a playground scene, he goes on to say,

All living things internalize and respond to dozens of rhythms. . . . The way in which people handle synchrony is both rooted in biology (bio-basic) and modified by culture. Synchrony or lack of it is an index of how things are going and can be an unconscious source of great tension when synchrony is low, absent, or of the wrong kind. (p. 79)

His chapter suggests that we will gain in our understanding of young children if we become sensitive to their rhythms, biological and cultural, as well as to our own. How would the social experience have differed if those babies had been prevented from banging their spoons, or if the chasing behavior of the wrestling 3-year-olds had been stopped?

4 Children's Protests
Emotional Moments

Throughout a young child's day-care day there are the inevitable brief moments of distress. The behaviors with which children and babies express themselves during these moments I am calling "children's protests," as opposed to more extended cries for help. The many small events that cause young children to show upset feelings often provide care givers with opportunities for learning about and teaching even the youngest in their charge. If you are an observer of a protest, you learn about the child. If you are in any sense a participant, the child is also learning something from and about you.

From the moment of birth children have the ability to make vigorous protest. I once helped in the care of a newborn who had to have blood drawn from his heel every hour. He not only cried briefly, but after the first time he kicked so vigorously that it took two people hanging onto him to perform this task.

When protests, which may often seem of only passing importance to a child or infant, are responded to, as in a give-and-take conversation, they become an experience in human communication. It is interesting that we talk even to the tiniest babies, not only by touching them but with words. "I know that hurt. I'm sorry, baby. You'll feel better soon." It is as though we automatically start practicing right away, expecting that the baby will begin to hear the music of our concern even though the words are meaningless. When we run counter to this impulse to respond positively to distress signals, if we ignore protests, just tolerate them, or automatically disapprove as though they are merely disruptive behavior, children may be getting many small lessons that tell them communication with adults is hardly worth their while.

41

In a group day-care situation, where one or two adults are caring for a number of children, protests present a particular challenge to the teachers. Children must not hurt each other. Also, a certain amount of conformity is necessary just to get through the routine of the day. The need to be changed or use the toilet, to eat, rest, and go outside, all may require a teacher ultimately to override protests. But there is another side to protests. They don't just challenge management and teaching skills. They provide a window into the inner lives of children, and for this reason they are to be treasured. There are quiet protests and vigorous protests. There are protests made with body language, protests made with cries, and protests made with words. Some are made with all three. However expressed, they all tell something about the ambitions, desires, fears, and interests of young children, which we as adults can learn from if we watch and listen, or if we take time to think about them after the crisis is past.

INFANTS: BOOK BATTING AND HAIR PULLING

In this particular infant toddler room the teacher had just finished going through a large picture book with three interested 9- and 10-month-olds. They were sitting among quilts and pillows on the floor. When finished, the teacher handed each baby his or her own book and started to get up, but before she could move, one little boy, Mikey, climbed into her lap, waving his book for more reading and saying, "Ba. Ba." The teacher opened the book, and once again he was focused intently on the pictures as she named them. One of the other children on the floor did not want the book she herself had, or any book as it turned out. Polly wanted the teacher's attention, telling her so by making a couple of little whimpering sounds, then by creeping up and batting the book that was being read. Mikey, the interrupted reader, quick as a flash grabbed a handful of the intruder's hair. She screeched. The teacher untangled fingers from hair saying, "Na, na, na, na. This is too rough," and repeating it once more as she looked carefully into the hair puller's face. Then she took his hand, making it stroke the crying Polly. While she did this she was saying in a gentle, drawn-out sing-song, "Niice. Niice." Then she smoothed back Mikey's hair from his forehead and pulled him up with his head next to hers and rocked him back and forth.

All this time she had been holding Polly in her other arm. By the end she was holding both children close and rocking them in a loving way. Then Polly went on to a bottle and a nap, which was what she was apparently ready for, while Mikey went cheerfully off to other business.

The wonderful thing about this scene was the confidence and vigor with which these two babies expressed their desires and needs. Here was an adult that they knew they could talk to, even though they had no words. And here was a teacher who talked back to them, matching her actions and words to their sounds and body language. The children also reached out to each other, whether intentionally or not, so it was a three-way conversation, the children trying ways to communicate and the teacher showing more acceptable alternatives. Each child wanted something from the teacher. And each child lashed out physically at the object seen as interference. Nine-month-old Polly, who could not wait for attention, told the teacher so by trying to get rid of the book. Mikey, on the other hand, was intently focused on the book. He appeared to want the teacher to put words to the pictures and was not just looking for her physical attention. The teacher held the injured Polly close, but her focus remained on Mikey. Perhaps she felt that she did not want to reward Polly for her aggressive action, and that teaching Mikey that hair pulling was unacceptable required her fuller attention. She seemed to think that he needed reassurance more than Polly.

If a group of teachers and parents were to look at the movie of this scene, they might focus on other aspects of the minidrama or have questions about each person's behavior. They might disagree altogether as to what was happening. But the point I wish to make is that a cluster of learning events was taking place around these moments of protest. The babies were learning something about cause and effect from their communications, while the teacher was learning about the two children's interests, attention span, competence, and ability to tolerate delay. You might argue that she already knew these things because she had been their teacher for 8 hours a day. Nevertheless, there is always more to learn at this age when children are changing so fast.

ONE-YEAR-OLDS: WAILING

SamSam, the child described in the following drama, was 14 months old. A teacher was seated on the floor blowing bubbles with a group of animated toddlers crowded around her. She had given each child an empty bubble jar and plastic blower stick to hold, so that those who were not having a turn with her blower, or catching bubbles, might also be involved. After a while there were only three children left around her, two on her lap trying to blow real bubbles and SamSam at her feet working with his empty jar and stick. Once he lost the stick inside the container and handed it to the teacher, screwing up his face and making little distress grunts. When she didn't understand the problem right away, he also began to wring his hands. It looked as though he would cry any second. However, she got the stick out just in time and handed stick and jar back to him.

After a few more minutes the teacher stood up. She announced that they were going to move into the playroom next door. "Let's go into the big room. Want to go into the big room, guys?" She held open a large plastic bag, telling the children to drop their bubble sticks and jars into it. They all did so with alacrity, seeming to be eager to go into the other room where there were balls and slides and climbing equipment. SamSam was the exception. Although he looked up a couple of times, he did not move. He continued to work on his project. When everyone else had gone out with the assistant, the teacher went over to him and squatted down. "Want to go to the big room? See the bird?"

SamSam looked up at her. He held up the stick and said softly, "Bubbles." All this time the teacher was holding the bag in front of her. "You want to play with the bubbles?" Pause. "You want to stay, or go into the big room?" SamSam said "Bubbles" again, looking up as though he wanted to share with her. "If you want to go into the big room, the bubbles stay right here." SamSam got up and toddled toward the door. "SamSam, SamSam put the bubbles in before you go in the big room." The teacher walked over quickly to squat down again, her body blocking the door. SamSam put his jar down. "That's right. The bubbles stay in the room." But instead of putting the jar in the bag, SamSam successfully got the stick in the jar. The teacher said with enthusiasm, "Good work!" SamSam then got to his feet and tried to go past her. Again he was blocked, although she didn't touch him. "If you want to go into the big room, the bubbles stay here." This whole scene was just a little less intense than it may sound because the teacher gave SamSam space and time carrying on a casual conversation about other matters with another teacher standing nearby. Finally SamSam slipped past her. She evidently did not want to continue to block his way, but once he was through the door she followed and took the jar from his hand to put in the bag. SamSam flung himself flat on the floor, tossing away the stick as he did so. He must have held his breath, for there was a second of silence and then an enormous wail of distress. The teacher didn't try to pick him up, but she was down there beside him to comfort and work it out as best she could.

Here the issues become more complex than in the hair-pulling episode. Clearly the teacher wanted to respond to the messages that SamSam was giving by his behavior and she took the time to do so. But what was he saying? And did the issues change during the course of the conversation? Did they each just want their own way? Certainly by the end they both clearly had different goals. SamSam wanted both the big room and his project. The teacher wanted him to choose between them. In a contest of wills, does the teacher have to win whenever possible? Can exceptions be made when there seems to be a reason, such as SamSam's interest in mastering a physical problem? Does making an exception to a rule that is not of critical importance mean that you are teaching a child that he, or she, does not have to do what you ask? The teacher could have said, "I see that this is really important to you, so I'm going to let you take the bubbles into the big room today. Please give them to me when you're finished." On the other hand, perhaps having that long conversation created the problem in the first place. Or perhaps SamSam always wanted to march to a different drum and the teacher felt that this was a good moment to tell him that sometimes she wanted things her way. Of course, there are no definitive answers to these questions. Each teacher and each parent faced with a protest will have a different style, a different set of circumstances, and a different child. But every time, something will be taught and something learned. So protests are opportunities. They are also puzzles that need solutions based on the messages they carry. And the messages do not necessarily get clearer as the children develop language. Often quite the opposite is true.

TWO-YEAR-OLDS: A RAISED VOICE

When I visited 2-year-old Marie in her center early one morning, I saw that she had brought two plastic lunch boxes to day care. She wanted to keep them with her at all times, but that meant laying them down here and there. Each time another child would pick one up, she would recapture it, crying out her indignation in a high, piercing voice accompanied by vigorous pulling. "That's mine. Give it back." And each time the teacher was in the middle of the drama. With a quiet voice she helped to retrieve the boxes. After a couple of these episodes Marie went to the sand table. When she discovered that she needed both hands free, she turned and waved one of the lunch boxes in the air, calling, "Here, Teacher. Here, teacher." The teacher, coming over and sitting down at her level, said, "How about if I put it on the counter so no one will take it?" "NO! Put it on the table." Marie pointed dramatically to the table behind her where one lunch box already was resting. "You know what, Marie, if you put it on the table someone will want to look at it. I can put it on the counter next to Toby's bottle?" Marie studied the situation for a second, then said, "Don't take it away."

Marie's teacher always spoke softly with spaces between her comments and made no sudden moves. While she was talking, she put the box Marie had handed to her on the table, as though to ease the tension. "In a couple of minutes we can put them on the counter." Here she paused and picked up one of the boxes. "Then perhaps we can go for a walk." At that moment there was a terrific screech from the sand table. Without having time to put the box down again the teacher stood up and moved to the screecher. Marie grabbed the box from under her teacher's arm. "I want to do it. I want to do it. I want to put this away." She appeared to be totally converted to the idea, marching with both boxes across the room to put them up on the counter where the food was prepared.

Marie's voice tones and shrill demands were not easy to hear. Her teacher, however, was able to respond to her protests as though

Marie were saying, "Can you hear me? Will you help me if I need you?" This question might well be asked by any young children through their behavior, although the behavior would likely be different for a 3- or 4-year old.

The point is that these smallest children separate from home and parent in many different ways. Some cry and cling. Some march off without showing us how the transition feels to them. Some have a transitional object and some, like Marie, also test the waters vigorously to be sure they can make themselves heard and understood. Although such a transition may be difficult for a teacher, it also can be very rewarding. It is a way for teacher and child to establish understanding and trust. The question is asked and the adult has a chance to answer.

THREE-YEAR-OLDS: BITING

Every child in this 3-year-old room was busily engaged by nine o'clock in the morning. Unlike the 2-year-olds in Marie's group, who were often clustered around their teacher, these children were primarily focused on each other with a lot of talk going on between them. Some children were eating at the table, some were playing house, and Jeffrey and his friend, Ralph, were over beside a high platform that was reached by a vertical ladder. Earlier I had seen a teacher helping Jeffrey to climb up and down that ladder. He was clearly afraid of falling even with the teacher holding him. Now he had set out a path of steering wheels below the platform, which he carefully walked, balancing from wheel to wheel. Ralph watched and then he walked the path in just the same way. Jeffrey was a child who often had the interesting ideas that other children followed, and Ralph was one of his followers.

After this game palled, Ralph started up the ladder. Jeffrey tried to dissuade him, even pulling at his shirt to hold him back. But Ralph persisted. Once up he turned and started taunting Jeffrey, who stood below on the second rung looking up. Ralph twirled and teased for a few minutes before deciding to come down, which he did facing forward and holding onto the rails. By this time Jeffrey was apparently so frustrated and furious that he bit Ralph on the knee when it was suddenly right in front of his nose.

There was one of those laden seconds of silence and then a great cry arose from Ralph. "He bite me." Teachers rushed over to the scene while Jeffrey, hastily looking around, walked away. When she had examined the assaulted knee, which was not seriously damaged, the teacher called Jeffrey over. He came quickly, looking up into her face as she told him, "You're not supposed to bite. Use your words." With that, Jeffrey turned and called loudly up to Ralph, who had remained on the platform, "I don't like that!" The teacher then said, "No, *he* doesn't like that." Then there was no further discussion and the boys went off in different directions.

Jeffrey, Ralph, and the teacher each had made a judgment about what had happened. Their perceptions were clearly different. Ralph was outraged, as well as slightly hurt, because one of the cardinal rules had been broken when his friend had bitten him. Perhaps he knew that he would get the teacher's sympathy. In any case, he knew it was an important infringement that needed to be reported. Jeffrey also knew that this impulsive bite was a forbidden behavior, but apparently he gave it a lower priority than his friend's betrayal. So when the teacher told him to use his words he went back to the moment before the bite to say, "I don't like that." The teacher appeared momentarily confused when she corrected Jeffrey by saying, "*He* doesn't like that." Perhaps she had expected him to say he was sorry. In any case, she made no further comment on the biting, undoubtedly remembering that she had neither seen nor heard the actual drama, or what led up to it. Her judgment was not to press charges. Should she have encouraged the children to talk about what happened, or about Jeffrey's fears and Ralph's feeling about always being his friend's follower? Or was it better to let them separate without emphasizing their quarrel and the reasons for it?

CONCLUSION

In each of the scenes I have described here, cultural concepts and children's feelings were interacting. In the first scene the babies were expressing themselves without inhibitions and the teacher was introducing a cultural rule: Hair pulling is too rough. In the second scene the toddler, SamSam, was learning what an adult role is and how much importance it is given. Perhaps he recognized from his teacher's voice tones and expression that this rule was not absolutely necessary, and was trying to tell her that his project was more important.

Marie with her lunch boxes was also learning about her culture by practicing what she had already learned. She was trying out the concept of personal property as a way of expressing her feelings. A less perceptive teacher might have thought she was being selfish, or needlessly, even mischievously, provocative. In a sense she was, yet her questions were valid and important. This is an example of a verbal child whose words do not tell the whole story.

As for the 3-year-olds in the final episode, they had moved into a far more socially complex realm where their interest was primarily in one another, not in the teacher. They knew the cultural taboo against biting. Jeffrey was willing to be reminded, and to practice without resentment a better way of expressing his anger. But he was more deeply concerned over the meanness of his friend. Although he felt the teasing was not right, the cultural rule was not so clear as the one about biting. By not making more of an issue over the bite, was the teacher confirming Jeffrey's judgment that mean teasing was unacceptable? Or, on the other hand, did she fail to teach him the seriousness of biting? One answer is that all of these issues become ongoing conversations between a teacher and the children in his or her charge. Because learning is a process, and one that is inevitably personal between teacher and child, having the same teacher rather than constant change is particularly important during these early years. Then when children fail to live up to what we are trying to teach, they need not be pounced upon or expected to learn everything at once. Then teachers as well as parents can have flexible margins of trial and error that give them time to understand their children's messages.

Once you start this type of examination of the small dramas, the *protests,* that are the everyday events of child care, it becomes clear that to teach these babies and young children the basic mores of their culture along with giving them self-confidence and a sense of security is a never-ending challenge. The issues are often complex, and there are no easy formulas to depend upon for problem solving. But if teachers and parents can keep in mind that the children are teaching them, as well as vice versa, the puzzles of growth and development need not seem formidable.

These puzzle protests are distinct from deep distress and hard crying, which are also central to the development of communication skills, social attitudes, and feelings about self and others. For this reason the next chapter will focus specifically on prolonged distress and crying.

OTHER VOICES

Parents and early childhood teachers are usually addressed separately. However, what is written for one group is often provocative material for both. This is true of Elaine Heffner's (1978) *Mothering*. In a chapter on mothers as teachers she writes,

> We have automatic reactions to certain behavior, and these reactions diminish our powers of observation. It is enormously difficult to set aside this emotional response in order to understand the real function the behavior is serving for the child. (p. 127)

She goes on to say,

> We have been so thoroughly conditioned to feel that certain behavior must not be permitted that our response is to try to stop it. If one tries to shift the focus from stopping it to understanding it, it feels as though nothing is being done about the behavior—the behavior is still there! This begins to seem like permitting it. (p. 127)

She has found in her many discussions with mothers,

> an almost universal assumption that understanding behavior means accepting it. In fact, it is just the other way around. It is only by understanding behavior that one can effectively do something about it. In order to know what to do, you first have to know what it is you are trying to do something about. The child's behavior signals where he is in his social development. (p. 127)

5   Crying
Lessons in Communication

When a child cries hard and long in day care, will someone be there who understands, and will that person be able to answer that particular child's need? These can be nagging questions for parents of infants and toddlers, and also for the parents of passionate children who express themselves easily with tears, or for parents of homesick children. But this is not merely an emotional issue for parents. It is a practical issue that has to do with early education at its very roots. When children in day care cry, what is taught? What is learned? What is considered desirable by our society?

CRYING AS COMMUNICATION

Because crying and communication are inevitably linked together in the earliest months and years, when crying is a dominant expressive behavior, this age is perhaps the best place to look for answers. Parents turn the cries of their new baby into a communication by responding to them. When crying produces a response that is empathetic, it is a positive experience in social learning for the baby, who comes to expect to be heard and understood. To start life with the resulting sense of trust and well-being sets the stage for most other desirable kinds of learning. Therefore, crying, and how it is handled, is crucial to any discussion about quality care outside of the home, particularly for the youngest children. Because we are a multicultural society, and because child-care workers have very different levels of training and experience, it is perhaps not surprising that we don't have a general agreement on how to handle crying in day-care centers. Some teachers treat crying, along with other child behaviors, as having valid meaning and respond as they would to a verbal message of distress. Others see it as just another aspect of immaturity that must be tolerated. Still others believe that crying is undesirable behavior, and that children should learn not to cry as soon as possible. But when preverbal children do not cry, that in itself can be a problem.

Silent Crying

The following episode describes a toddler who didn't cry or ask for help when he was feeling upset. Early one morning I watched the mother of this 13-month-old boy saying good-bye at the door of the nursery. She was clearly reluctant to leave. He stayed focused on her but did not cry or try to hold onto her, so I was more aware of her discomfort than of his. After the door closed, the child tipped forward in a kind of toddler run, moving at random across the floor. The teacher, who had greeted mother and child from across the room and had apparently been watching, suddenly got up from where she was sitting with two other toddlers. When she moved swiftly to pick up this little boy, I saw then that his mouth was wide open and his eyes appeared glazed. Since there were other teachers in the room, she was able to retreat to the rocking chair, and for 10 minutes she held the child with the silent cry until his face brightened and he was ready to get down. You might say that this child's silence was a step in the right direction, that he was learning to cope and be independent. However, when not crying means not trying to communicate, that certainly is undesirable behavior for this age.

Shared Feelings

Within the family a child's feelings of misery and of delight, and everything in between, are stimulants for their developing communication skills. In day care, when teachers fail to respond to crying in positive ways, it is at the very least an opportunity missed, and an isolating rather than a socializing experience for the child. Once children can talk they are usually urged to speak out if they have a problem. However, for the preverbal child, when going off to day care feels too hard, he or she can best make the point by crying. Most need to do this from time to time if they are to share their distress with parent or teacher.

A Wrinkle in Time

One special complication is that many children arrive at their day-care centers before they have had breakfast, and having to eat away from home can be upsetting for some at this age. In addition, separations are often painful, and transitions themselves are difficult. Although this process of moving out into a larger world is inevitable and necessary for learning, it has some special features for small infants and toddlers who go to child-care centers. For them, this move is a kind of wrinkle in time, a jump unaccompanied by developmental readiness for independence from a mother or other primary person. Giving these children the lesson that they can be heard and understood in this larger day-care world is part of what makes it feel safe to them. It is also the key to keeping their learning on a developmental continuum with the average, caring home. For when infants and toddlers, as well as older children, experience the human environment in which they spend so much time as responsive in positive ways, they are laying good foundations for communication skills. This is a major reason why crying times are important.

The Teacher's Dilemma

Unfortunately not all teachers know how to deal with the management of crying children in a group situation. There is the false assumption often made by parents, and by teachers themselves, that the very fact of being in the teacher role automatically means knowing a right way to act toward a crying child. Of course this is not true. Teachers don't always know what to do, any more than parents always know how to cope with every situation.

There is a basic dilemma that always faces the day-care teacher. Seen from the teacher's vantage point, no matter how he or she would interact with children singly, that teacher has to decide if it is possible to nurture the individual to the same degree in group care. Is it desirable to address the crying of one child in ways that might produce further communications of the same sort from that child, or is the teacher's primary goal supposed to be the adjustment of the individual to the needs of the group? The day-care teacher has to think about whether the very fact of having these children in a group means that the social design for them must be the same as for school-age children, along with similar expectations of behavior. In other words, he or she has to decide what skills the children are actually supposed to be learning and what is supposed to be taught. This makes the teachers specially vulnerable to trends such as the present one towards social conformity in day care, which goes hand in hand with the pressure for more academic types of learning. Today, this trend reaches right down into infant/toddler programs, sometimes into the very cribs of day care. I have seen a number of situations that illustrate just how difficult the problem of crying can be for day-care teachers.

NAP TIMES

The Crying Nap

Late one afternoon I visited a day-care center that had only recently opened an infant/toddler program. There was a separate room for napping with windowed doors at each end, one opening into the nursery and one into the hall. As I approached from this outer side, I could hear some very hard crying. Looking through the window into the darkened sleeping space, I saw that it was arranged with double-decker cribs along one wall. To keep the children from falling, these usually have nets that fasten down over the outer side. In this instance there was also a light blanket covering the opening of one of the bottom cribs so that it must have been entirely dark inside. It was from this crib that the cries were coming. The net was evidently tied in place because the blanket bulged and shook in accompaniment with the cries, but no child emerged. I went to look for the teachers and found two young women sitting on the nursery floor chatting together and playing with another baby in what looked like an idyllic end-of-the-day scene except for the loud crying from next door, which continued for another 15 minutes. When I asked the teachers what was happening, they explained to me that they were doing what the mother had told them to do, and that this 10-month-old baby always had to cry himself to sleep. Presumably there was some special reason for their wanting him to take such a late nap.

"Children Must Sleep"

In our society a rather inflexible tradition of naps has come to be accepted in most child-care situations, as though napping at a given time were as natural and inevitable as a child's need to urinate, eat, or drink. Of course young children get tired in a long day, but just how rigid should these schedules actually be, either for infants and toddlers or for older children?

In most day-care centers if you ask about the children who do not sleep, you will usually be told that everybody sleeps. In fact, groups of children do accept a regular sleeping time. Many children need and want naps. Others learn to sleep at the desired times without trauma, or can be trained, if not to sleep, to lie more or less quietly in a darkened room for up to 2 hours. But what about the exceptions who resist naps? Isn't it overdoing conformity to penalize them?

Because teachers need time off and our limited funds for space and staff make it difficult to be flexible, this practical problem has been transformed in many instances into a developmental theory. The groups in day care are often large and the staff usually as small as the law will allow. And because teachers need a rest, it has been rationalized that children must all need a nap time after lunch. For the verbal children, this means that they are a nuisance, if not actually regarded as "bad" when they do not sleep or remain quiet. For nonverbal children, this nap-time theory can mean confinement and tears if they do not want or need a nap at the same time as the others.

There are alternatives to nap times for nonsleepers. One solution came from a group of parents who got together and volunteered to each give two lunch hours a month to run a permanent room for quiet play during naps. This took the pressure off children and teachers alike, although only a few children used the room at any given time. These were usually toddlers who had fallen asleep while being trundled home from a morning trip and who were not ready to sleep again. This arrangement would not work for every center, but it demonstrates that it is possible to create more flexible programs.

MEALTIMES

Crying at Breakfast

Mealtimes are also sensitive times in day care, with babies and the youngest children especially vulnerable. Learning to eat is a complex process that can be frustrating for young children when they are hungry, tired, or homesick. Mealtimes are difficult for teachers, too, when children are upset. It is easy to imagine a scenario in which a baby who fusses and won't eat his breakfast is simply picked up and comforted, or distracted in some way from his unhappiness. It is harder to imagine what happens when a teacher does not know how to do this. The following description is of an episode in which the teacher did not know how to respond to crying in a positive way. It demonstrates in the extreme the kind of misunderstanding that can arise around methods and goals in regard to crying.

In this particular program there were 16 infants and young toddlers in a large, rather carelessly organized room. When I first arrived it was early morning, so only about half the group were present, with three adults in attendance. The toddlers and babies old enough to sit up were having breakfast around two low tables. The lighting was dim, the tables were crowded together in a small kitchen corner, and the atmosphere seemed generally strained. It quickly became obvious why. The head teacher was trying unsuccessfully to get one small boy to sit up and eat his breakfast. He was crying and kept sliding down in his chair. Each time that she pulled him back up to a sitting position he would slither down again. Finally the teacher pulled him up out of his seat altogether and carried him across the room to a giant fenced area set up in the middle of the floor. For the next 10 minutes the room was almost entirely silent except for the spasmodic crying of this child, whom I later learned was 9 months old. He lay on his back inside the fence and made no attempt to contact any of his teachers, nor did they call out to him.

Because most people are on their best professional behavior when being observed on the job, I assume the head teacher, who had given me permission to visit, was handling this child's crying in what she thought to be the most correct fashion under the circumstances. This meant to me that she was confused about basic developmental issues regarding the meaning of crying and how to respond to it. When she finally went to the child, she picked him up and carried him back across the room to the breakfast table, explaining to him as she did so that he could not stay at the table if he cried. Given the emotional context this came out as a threat. When she tried to sit him in his chair he arched his back, starting to cry again. Her response was to return him to the play pen.

By now other children who had finished their meal were placed on the floor beside him. Even though this was temporarily distracting, when the head teacher left the room the baby immediately noticed and began to cry even harder, as though lost without her. The remaining teachers did not go to him. They were busy changing diapers and may also have thought that action on their part would be interference. In any case, the head teacher returned very shortly and took the baby into the now empty alcove where they had breakfast together. It was a sober affair with no socializing. I think both teacher and child were exhausted by their failure to communicate with each other more successfully.

Bad Behavior

Whether her beliefs were drawn from her own background or from poor professional training, this teacher apparently thought that a simple, warm response on her part would be a mistake and would teach this child all sorts of bad things: to be defiant, or willful, or always to cry for what he wanted. It has been my experience that children often cry because they expect in advance not to be understood, but will tolerate all kinds of discomforts once they are confident that they are heard and that someone will try to understand. Crying is not "bad" behavior. It always means something and in that sense it is a communication. Older children will often be equally unable to tell the teacher what is actually bothering them when they feel upset. However, they can complain of a stomachache or make some other verbal statement to announce their distress, whereas the preverbal child's most direct method of communication is through crying. When the teacher of infants and toddlers fails to see that crying as a distress signal has as much validity as the spoken word, then there is confusion instead of communication.

Developmental Age

Misjudgment of age is a problem in day care when teachers well trained for working with young children are not available, or when experienced teachers succumb to outside pressures for certain kinds of conforming behavior, and forget how immature their small charges still are. In the case just described, the teacher, having no words from the child to guide her, focused on teaching him that he could not cry at the table. And she did it as though she were trying to teach table manners to a much older child, using removal from the group as a method. This kind of time-out approach is seldom a successful way of teaching very young children. Even if they understand why they are being removed from the scene, the method easily gets mixed up with ideas of punishment, both in the child's mind and in the teacher's.

Dependence and Independence

When communication with children is closed off, the result is apt to be increasing dependency rather than advancing social skills and independence. A crying baby who feels he has made himself understood, or at very least has gotten someone to try to understand him, has had a successful lesson in communication, even if his problem is not immediately solved. But for a crying baby who gets no positive response, the world is a more dangerous place. If added to that, his cries bring down on him the strong disapproval of his primary teacher, he may need her constant presence in order to feel safe, or he may turn away from her altogether. These littlest children can be trained by negatives eventually not to cry, but if children are going to learn to be able to speak out, and in turn to listen to the concerns of others, then the nursery is the place to begin, with crying treated as a significant language.

Positive Responses

In another center I observed a teacher who continued to serve six other children breakfast while an 11-month-old boy was crying over separation from his parent. The teacher had him on a chair beside her, putting her hand lightly on his head from time to time with an acknowledging kind of gesture. She served him his meal along with the others, and each time there was a break in his crying she popped a spoonful into his mouth. He clearly wanted the food even though he continued to be upset.

The rest of the children were quiet and solemn, but more concerned with a baby crying across the room than with the child in front of them. Several repeatedly turned around in their seats in an attempt to see what was happening out of their sight. When breakfast was over, each child was given a bottle to take where he or she wished, a part of their daily routine. The teacher then turned her total attention to the crying child, taking him onto her lap and cuddling him while he drank his bottle. She was telling this child on the one hand that she accepted his message and that she sympathized, and on the other hand that everything was going to be all right, and that life would proceed in familiar ways. She was focused on responding to the message of distress rather than on the way it was being transmitted. You might say, "But what about the other children? Wasn't it unfair to make them sit through breakfast with such disruption?" Perhaps, but I suspect that they too were learning that if they felt unhappy their teacher would hear and accept their message, that she would take care of them.

This particular approach worked for this teacher and this child. Other teachers might have had to find different ways of handling the problem. For example, another teacher might have found it too stressful to sit through a meal with all that crying, or have decided it was too stressful for the rest of the children. He or she might have tried carrying the child around—perhaps to look out a window—or sitting with him in a rocking chair, letting breakfast wait. To be a successful problem solver with a crying child, each teacher must choose his or her own responses according to the circumstances, according to the teacher's own personality, training, experience, and according to what he or she knows about the child. Nevertheless, it helps to have thought about this problem in advance and to have some guidelines for the final results one wants to achieve.

ADAPTING TO DAY CARE

Along with upset feelings concerned with sleeping and eating, separating from parents can be particularly painful, as described in the last vignette, and there are no easy formulas for comforting a homesick child. Because these moments of distress are moments of learning, this is an added challenge for teachers. The following scene demonstrates what may be taught and what learned when crying is not treated as a valid communication.

The Wading Pool

It was summertime in this middle-class European center when I visited, and the children were all outside. During the first part of the morning the infant/toddler group was in a large sandbox area. Then they moved to a grassy section of their yard where the teachers had filled a giant plastic wading pool. One baby about 8 or 9 months old had been sitting on the edge of the sand area crying hard off and on for 20 minutes. Without knowing the language, I was unable to ask what was happening. Perhaps the child was new at the center and they felt that continuous comforting would only prolong his adjustment, or perhaps he was upset for some other reason and they had tried to comfort him and been rejected. Whatever the cause of his distress, it was striking that neither the other children nor the teachers seemed to notice the crying. When everyone moved off to the wading pool, the baby continued to be ignored, but he crawled after them anyway.

The water play was a wonderful sight. By now the 2- and 3-year-olds had come out, so there were 15 children in all. They were allowed to drop their clothes on the grass and jump into the water naked. There was much enjoyment and splashing, particularly by the older children and two of the teachers, who had put on bathing suits. Splashing was encouraged. The children were clearly being taught to enjoy getting their faces wet. Although some of the youngest were a bit cautious, it was still a free and happy scene except for the crying baby.

One teacher, apparently feeling that she should finally do something for this miserable child, suddenly scooped him up from behind. He was unprepared, as she had made no eye contact or other communication before approaching him. Instead, within seconds his diaper was pulled off and he was placed in the pool. Although the teacher held him securely around the chest with one hand, this attention did nothing to calm him, and when she splashed water over his face and head, his screams became hysterical. A few children glanced over briefly, but then returned to their play, seeming to take their cue from the adults that this baby did not need their sympathy. The teacher's response to his cries was to plop him back down on the grass and turn away in obvious frustration. The baby, now howling, crawled after her, and when he got close held up his arms toward her retreating back.

At this point a visiting parent stepped forward. While talking to the baby she slowly picked him up. Her attentions calmed him a little until another staff member came out of the building and carried him away. The involved teacher was obviously relieved. Evidently she was following some policy at the center to discourage crying by ignoring it, and she herself was unable to make variations on the rule. The parent, on the other hand, perceived this child's distress signals as so critical that she was willing to step out of the usually passive role of visitor.

The Group Lesson

I am not forgetting that the above example of teacher behavior was drawn from an entirely different culture from our own. It is, however, similar enough so that I believe the same basic principles hold true about how young children learn to communicate, and how the response to crying plays an important role. The rest of the children in this play yard were being taught by example not to respond to human distress signals. The baby himself was learning that he could not make himself heard when he was in need. It is doubtful that this could lead him to have compassion for others. The center was probably trying to teach children to be independent, and cheerful, and had some theory that any sympathetic attention to crying of this sort would have the opposite effect. Apparently they had not thought about the social learning that might be picked up by the whole group when a crying child is ignored, not to mention the negative lesson for the baby.

CONCLUSION

Being left to cry for short periods is part of the ongoing dialogue about needs and wishes that takes place between children and their parents in almost every home. It can happen when children don't want to go to bed, or don't want their mother to go into the bathroom and close the door. Nevertheless, I believe it is definitely not a safe practice in day-care centers, where children are away from home in the charge of a changing staff with varying education and judgment. What was that baby learning about himself and others as he lay on the floor and cried during breakfast? And did confining the other toddler in a totally dark space really differ from shutting a child in a closet? I have never seen a crying verbal child in day care forcibly confined in a room alone, although I have seen children sent out of a room to cry. Solitary confinement would generally be considered unacceptable, and confinement in a dark room would be considered shocking. Yet I have been in nurseries a number of times where the gentlest teachers seemed to feel that it was right to leave a preverbal child confined and crying in a sleeping-room. It is a special problem for the youngest day-care children if their teachers believe that what would be considered extreme, punitive, and unsafe behavior toward a verbal child is somehow acceptable if applied to a baby who cannot talk.

For these reasons, although many care givers may feel it impractical, I believe that no crying child or baby should ever be left unattended in a child-care program. I believe we could avoid these negative experiences if it were widely understood that teachers should always respond positively to the emotional message of crying as though to words, and with nonpunitive solutions.

OTHER VOICES

Ben S. Bradley (1989) has a chapter called "Infancy and Paradise" in his book, *Visions of Infancy*. He says,

> The vision of infancy as bliss can only be maintained if scientists condone a selective blindness to the negative aspects of babyhood, aspects which emerge all too quickly once one considers as a whole the daily life of babies and those who look after them. I make this argument in order to sketch an alternative vision of infancy—as a struggle to transcend ambivalence. (p. 170)

He is referring here to those moments of ambivalence in care givers that result in hardship for babies. Bradley points out that research into how and what babies learn tends to focus on infant development in laboratory situations, with healthy babies and cooperating mothers. He is concerned that this does not represent the learning that is apt to take place in the hurly-burly of everyday life. There is another side to the story of babyhood and early learning that should also be heard, one that is not so ideal and is affected by all the social, economic, sexual, and political pressures on the principal care giver.

The day-care worker, of course, comes with his or her own set of life stresses. What parent or teacher has not experienced a moment of ambivalence when faced with responsibility for a baby who will not or cannot stop crying? So even where there is no carelessness, insensitivity, ignorance, or life-threatening environment, babies must struggle.

6 Social Values
"Mine" and "Ours"

Social values are hard to pin down in any discussion, because they are so patently subjective and culture bound. For example, some adults stress strict adherence to rules, whereas others have quite different priorities. However, because social values are inevitably part of the responses of teachers to children, the role they play in day care cannot be ignored.

Babies and young children are like blotting paper, absorbing all the attentions that their parents offer. When they go into child-care programs, their teachers' behaviors are added to parent behaviors that tell them about other people. These are the behaviors based upon attitudes and beliefs, and rules for living together, loosely referred to here as social values. From this constant flow of teacher responses the children learn how to interpret the approaches of others, what to expect, how to respond.

The influence of teacher values on social learning can often be seen particularly clearly in infant/toddler groups. There are several reasons for this. For one thing, the care of children under 2 requires a kind of quiet concentration on the minutiae of living. The teachers necessarily focus on small events in the here and now, with the result that there are few hidden references to past or future that would make it difficult for the observer to understand the teacher/child exchanges. Attitudes and beliefs, usually not stated explicitly, become observable in very concrete ways during teacher interactions with infants and toddlers. This is particularly true just because teachers must meet preverbal children more than halfway in social exchange. They set the priorities as they teach babies and toddlers how to interact with their environment.

The following events, drawn from my observations in two contrasting centers, demonstrate how this works, how teacher values lead to teacher behaviors, which, in turn, transmit observable messages to children. The programs differed in group size, teacher/child ratios, backgrounds of the children, and physical settings. Although each of these two centers had skillful teachers who worked closely with their center directors, it was easy to see that the two sets of teachers were transmitting fundamentally separate messages about how human beings live together. The two groups of toddlers already looked and acted in ways that were observably different from one another.

SUBURBAN CENTER

The Setting

The first center was located in a church basement on a tree-lined street in suburbia. It served white, upwardly mobile, professional families almost exclusively. The infant/toddler room had two teachers and six children ranging in age from 7 to 14 months.

The feeding arrangement consisted of a low table built along one wall. The children were lifted into place at mealtimes, sitting on a bench between wall and table. This design made socializing possible between child and child as well as between teacher and child. The teachers sat on the floor with the children lined up in front of them. They could reach out to help the children, who on their part had readily available eye contact with their teachers. Also each child could easily touch whoever was sitting next to him or her.

Snack Time

One day 13-month-old Carol was sitting next to 12-month-old Jeannie at snack time. The children had been given slices of bread. Carol took her piece and held it up to Jeannie's mouth. Jeannie opened her mouth a little when the bread touched her lips, but that was as far as they were able to get. They remained in this pose for several seconds as though trying to understand what was happening. The teacher laughed but made no other comment. Next Carol reached over and took a piece of apple that was in front of Jeannie. This time the teacher commented carefully on the event. "That's Jeannie's apple. Can you give it back to her?" She repeated this several times, finally taking the apple gently from Carol's hand and returning it to Jeannie. In this situation the teacher didn't encourage social interaction between the children, choosing to focus instead on which piece of apple belonged to which child. She did this with questions and explanations rather than with directions and admonitions, physically helping the year-old Carol to carry out the desired behavior.

Property Rights

Here was an attitude or belief system at work that stressed the concept of individual ownership over and above sharing, or at least over an experimental social gesture of one child toward another. Although this incident might be seen as a simple case of teaching the table manners that make it possible for people to eat together, an equally acceptable scenario might have stressed Carol's social gesture, with the teacher saying something like, "I see you are giving Jeannie some bread." However, it gradually became evident that this teacher brought property rights, or what one might call property identification, into almost every interaction that she had with the children.

For example, one day the same two children were sitting outdoors in the sandbox with the teacher, among a welter of pails, shovels, and sieves. Carol took a pail from Jeannie and Jeannie began to cry. This time it took some minutes of unscrambling, with the teacher carefully clarifying each child's relationship to objects and people. "Carol, Jeannie was playing with that." "Jeannie, if you're going to use that you can give Carol this." Again the teacher appeared to be teaching awareness of self and other, through the allocation of objects, giving this lesson priority over other possible choices such as digging a hole together or focusing on the sand.

On still another occasion Jeannie took 10-month-old Patrick's bowl as they sat playing with the teacher on the floor. The teacher had been showing them how to stir with spoons, saying, "Helping me cook?" When Jeannie took Patrick's bowl, Patrick hit her with a spoon. The teacher first addressed the property rights issue. "Jeannie, Patrick is playing with that now." Second she addressed the aggressive gesture. "Patrick, you don't need to hit." In each of these instances the interactions ended with the children turning away from each other. Was this because value was placed primarily on the object, with the social contact not treated as being of any particular interest?

Self-Identification

The atmosphere in this group was a leisurely, quietly verbal one in which teacher/child rather than child/child contacts were the norm. Although the teacher used a lot of positive language in talking to the children, what she taught them, in effect, was how to identify personal property. She used the group situation to strengthen each child's awareness of self, but in a way that did not foster interest between the children or promote any pleasurable interactions among them.

Of course, this identification of self through relation to the physical environment is a universal component of early and of ongoing human experience. Under what most people in our society would consider to be good conditions, a baby has his or her own primary person, parent, or parents, own home, own sleeping place, own food, clothes, and toys, not to mention own body, to use in identifying self. It is important to have some simulation of this experience for the development of institutionalized children, if they are to become normally functioning members of society. Were the teachers in the suburban center perhaps trying to make up to the children for not being at home, for being in a sense institutionalized? Or were they rather reflecting in their behavior a cultural belief that property rights are even more important than empathy for, or interest in, one's neighbor at this age? To the degree that it is necessary to be aware of self in order to be truly aware of others, they were, of course, correct.

URBAN CENTER

The Setting

The second center was located in an urban housing development. The youngest group there had three teachers taking care of 15 black, oriental, and white children between the ages of 4 months and 14 months.

The area set aside for the infant/toddler program was one section of a very large space that also served two older age-groups. Each of these groups had a vista into other spaces, so the children could interact with each other, or with the teachers in the adjoining spaces. Necessarily the noise level was high.

Mealtime

On a day when seven of the 1-year-olds were all seated and waiting for lunch, two of the children began to bang their hands on the table top. The others picked it up. Then, adding to the play, one child said, "Da!" This was imitated too. Next four boys and girls, one following the other, pointed at the window and the remaining three followed with their eyes. These children were actively stimulated by being together. You could almost say they were having a conversation.

All the babies in this urban program who were old enough to sit up at a round table with low chairs. (This was the same table and group that I talked about in Chapter 3 in the discussion of rhythm, repetition, and imitation.) Whereas the shape of the table surely influenced the children's behavior at meal time, it was part of a general atmosphere that encouraged social contacts between toddlers. As the children faced each other they imitated each other, but more significant for their social development, they looked as if they enjoyed each other.

Group Identification

It began to appear that mealtime here reflected and reinforced teacher values that were almost opposite to those in the suburban center just described. For instance, the teacher spoke very little.

Often the noise level in the big room would have made it difficult to have the kind of running adult commentary heard in the suburban center. But the children's socializing was not discouraged, either by voice or gesture. If anything, the teacher strengthened their sense of being a group by the way that she passed around the food. She did so in the rhythmic and patterned fashion discussed in Chapter 3, serving everyone in quick succession. When she did speak, she tended to give directions and praise, using single words such as "No" and "Good" for guideposts. Unlike the suburban teacher who gave many explanations as well as opportunities for choice, this urban teacher asked few questions and gave virtually no explanations. I found that these behavior patterns in both groups of teachers and children held true over a period of several months.

In this center, materials were also used in ways that emphasized the group instead of the individual, which was another marked difference from the suburban program where there tended to be more one-on-one teacher/child involvement with a book or toy. When the urban children were at a loose end, they were usually attracted into a group activity by one of the teachers. For example, a teacher sitting on the floor would start blowing soap bubbles and the children would gather around to chase or pop them. Everyone could participate in this project. Even the babies too young to sit up or crawl would be there in a teacher's lap or in a bouncing chair unless they were sleeping.

Sharing

During one such group activity the teachers had dumped a great collection of giant plastic beads on the floor. The babies and toddlers crawled around collecting, dumping, and trying to pull beads apart or, with the help of an adult, fasten them together. This clustering and use of one kind of material for all again fostered imitation among the children along with the sense of being part of a group. There were always enough beads for everyone, but one day a toddler inevitably pulled a bead chain out of another child's hands. Twelve-month-old Darren objected to having his chain taken and tried roughly to pull it back. The teacher then turned to him and said, "Can't you share?" She evidently used the word *share* in the sense of not being possessive about objects. The suburban teacher would probably have spoken first to Child One, explaining that the beads at that moment belonged to Child Two and then addressed Child Two, explaining that he didn't need to snatch. Learning to share was not prominent on the suburban agenda. It is tempting to take sides and defend one approach or the other, but my purpose here is simply to show how different teacher behaviors express differences in basic social values.

The small event with the beads documents graphically the teacher attitudes toward property rights in this particular urban center. Individual, temporary, ownership rights were given a very low priority, if indeed they were considered at all. Sharing, on the other hand, was given high priority, being both taught overtly and encouraged tacitly wherever it occurred. For instance, one of the babies still being fed in a high chair had been given a handful of Cheerios on her tray while she waited for a meal. Two of the toddlers saw this and came over to help her eat them. They had to reach up and fish for the cereal piece by piece. The baby watched these hands appearing over the edge of her tray at first with some doubt in her expression and then with mild interest. It was clearly a pleasant occasion for the two toddlers. The baby in the high chair saw no reason to object, the teachers no reason to interrupt. So this was a lesson in "It is all right to share."

Touching

Preventing aggressive behavior in the form of body contact was also given a high priority here. Unlike the suburban teachers, the urban center teachers always addressed an aggressive act first, regardless of circumstances, although the children in both places were generally discouraged in different ways from touching each other. If the urban babies who had just graduated to a stable sitting position began pulling or thumping on one another as they sat on the floor of the nursery, the teachers simply separated them physically. When they got a little older, they were reprimanded, as in one instance that I saw.

On this day, a teacher and two babies were sitting together. The teacher had just been hugging the 8-month-old in an intimate moment of play. Margot, the second child, who was 11 months old, watched with great interest until the hugged baby was again alone.

Then, imitating the teacher, she tried hugging the other baby herself. Her hug was clumsy and experimental and he began to cry. The teacher turned on her reprovingly. "Look what you did!" This was a lesson in "Don't touch," not a lesson in how to touch, or how to touch gently.

Friendship

Because these teacher responses discouraged children from attaching themselves to objects, even as temporary personal property, and from body contact with each other, the urban children became remarkably good at being together without conflict. Whether this was the result of a conscious teacher technique or not, it had some specific benefits for the children. First of all, it helped to make up for the comparatively low level of individualized attention from primary teachers, unavoidable in such a large group. The suburban toddlers in their smaller groups were able to have prolonged exchanges with their teachers when not engaged on their own. Lacking this degree of social contact with adults, the urban toddlers turned to each other. Those who could walk formed a clique that incorporated new walkers as they got onto their feet. During the course of a day these toddlers grouped and regrouped into little clusters of parallel activity, clearly aware of one another. The next vignette demonstrates their level of awareness and response to peers.

One morning a 13-month-old child was picked up and removed from a place where he had been told several times not to climb. The teacher had at first called out from across the room, "Tyler, no!" He was trying to get from the top of the climbing steps down into an adjoining crib. Two children who were near him reacted to his situation. They were both sitting at the bottom of the steps, each with a book. First they turned their heads to watch the drama above them. When the climber was finally removed, one of the children on the steps shook his book vigorously, got up, and walked away. The other child threw her book equally vigorously onto the floor and, after staring fixedly at the forbidden spot, began to climb toward it, then slowly she backed down again and she too left the area.

With this kind of peer involvement, the toddlers learned fast from watching each other interact with the teachers and the physical environment. In addition, their human environment was stabilized by their sense of closeness to age-mates in a day-care situation where adults were interchangeable and new faces were often introduced, particularly toward the end of the day when volunteers arrived to help. They had each other as familiar human constants, perhaps giving and getting the kind of pleasure and support one gets from standing next to a friend in a noisy crowd.

Independence

Finally, the social precociousness of the urban infant/toddlers gave them a certain freedom from continual adult intervention. On the one hand, this meant a less varied learning experience through teacher enrichment than in the suburban group. On the other hand, there was the definite sense that the children had a life of their own that had some independence within this large group situation. In spite of an occasional example of a child's being physically removed from a forbidden situation, these 1-year-olds were generally given the message by their teachers that they were competent and could exercise considerable control over their own bodies. This was a place where they could get up from the table and walk around when they were finished eating as soon as they were coordinated enough to maneuver out of a low cube-chair.

CONCLUSION

In summary, the suburban children got a great deal of teacher attention, with approximately as much exposure to language and other forms of symbolic materials, such as books and fantasy, as they might have had in their own homes, given their particular backgrounds. On the other hand, despite the greater intimacy of the group, the children needed a lot of teacher supervision if they got too close together, appearing to find each other threatening. Also, their teachers' emotional responses to them were so bland, even though positive, that the children's attachment to and interest in the teachers seemed equally bland, even impersonal. They learned a sense of self through "mine" and "thine," rather than connection.

By contrast, the urban children had greater independence and less exposure to language and symbolic materials. Their social relation to peers was more advanced and enjoyable, and their teachers' responses, whether negative or positive, were more warm, vigorous, and clear. All this may have been true in part because of the noise level in the room, and because there was less time for leisurely, individual teacher/child interactions. Whether these children with their strong group identification were getting enough nourishment for developing an equally strong sense of self and whether they were getting enough cognitive stimulation are other questions.

Both these programs had real strengths. My examination of them is not intended to criticize or judge one program to be better than the other. Nor am I trying to prescribe what values children should learn in day care. Rather, I want to demonstrate that social values, whether consciously or unconsciously, are being taught in every day-care program, and that they can be identified and discussed.

OTHER VOICES

Vivian Gussin Paley (1984), an experienced teacher, gives many striking examples of teacher awareness of values in *Boys and Girls—Superheroes in the Doll Corner*. When she writes, she takes the reader into her classroom, or nursery, by giving long sequences of the children's own voices, with enough action described to place the reader by her side. She also shares her thoughts about what is happening in the complex world that she is orchestrating. As a result, we see the process by which she learns and we can learn along with her.

Exploring how preconceptions affect attitudes toward the behaviors of girls, as opposed to the behaviors of boys, she writes,

My tolerance for running is directly related to what the runner is pretending and not to noise or distance covered.

Sisters chasing kittens, yelling and meowing, play out their scene and run back to the doll corner. Nor do I often interrupt ladies running in high heels, screaming with laughter. Skipping princesses arguing over a red velvet cape receive extra chasing time before arbitration is imposed.

However, the boy who runs out of the block corner with a Tinker Toy gun in hand is stopped abruptly. He is not noisier than an escaping kitten, but he sounds more violent. He probably has less aggressive intent than the girls grabbing the red cape, but his fantasy makes me uneasy. (p.35)

Having pinpointed her own bias, she goes on to show how the children themselves are reflecting and formulating values, ones that are not necessarily hers. For example, when she tells her group that the room is too noisy, one of the girls says that it is the boys who are noisy. When she replies that the girls are noisy in the doll corner, the same child tells her that the boys are noisier. She disagrees. At this point two of the boys join the conversation. One announces proudly that boys' shoes are heavier, while the other adds that boys make more noise because they have stronger feet than girls.

Paley's books are always sensitive to values, her own and the children's whom she teaches. Although this particular book is about a kindergarten class, the same kinds of observations can be made about infant/toddler groups. In fact, with her unusual self-awareness, she is a particularly relevant model for teachers of infant/toddler groups, because these children so readily reflect care-giver values, as shown in the infant/toddler programs that I have just described.

7 A Teacher's View
Maria

Wherever I visited a day-care room that seemed to be a busy, comfortable place, I asked the teachers to tell me how they created this atmosphere. Their answers not only helped me to understand what I was seeing but also gave me some insight into the invisible ingredients that make a program a nourishing experience for children. Clearly teacher attitudes and feelings are important.

When I interviewed Maria she was teaching in an infant/toddler program in California. A single parent in her early 30s, she was supporting two school-age children on a salary just above minimum wage. She was born in Mexico and had some training there in early education, as well as some experience teaching 3-year-olds, and was currently taking night courses at a big city college near her home.

At first I was confused by what I saw of Maria's program. Perhaps this was due in part to her flamboyant style, or to a cultural background that was unfamiliar to me. As an observer I always ask myself whether I would like to be a baby or child in a given place, and in the case of Maria's room the answer was definitely "Yes." But it was only after I had made several visits that I began to see why. She was combining important aspects of the two programs that I described in the last chapter, managing both to nurture the individuals in her group and at the same time to create the feeling among the children that they belonged together. She was also making more regular physical contact with each child than was evident in either of the other programs.

Although Maria was always neat and attractive in appearance, there were dramatic variations in the way she looked as well as in her mood. Sometimes she wore subdued colors, sometimes bright colors such as matching red pants and top. Sometimes she wore makeup and sometimes none. In the same way she could be very quiet, or she could be animated, noisy, and laughing. Another aspect of Maria's physical presence was the way she used her body. She could get down on the floor and up again so smoothly that the floor was as much her natural milieu as the children's, despite routines that made it necessary for her to be on her feet a great deal. She was on the floor to help, to comfort, to correct, to do special activities that she had planned, and to relax and play with the children.

A floor orientation is naturally characteristic of skilled teachers for this age group. In other ways the infant/toddler programs that I have seen tend to be quite different one from another. This particular group had the special characteristic of being more isolated than most. The director of Maria's center was also responsible for two other centers. Primarily an administrator, she was not a regular visitor in Maria's nursery room. The educational director was equally busy elsewhere because she had to attend to the daily operating details for all the different groups. So Maria with one assistant ran a program that was largely her own creation. For this reason I hoped that she could answer questions about her goals and purposes with greater clarity than a teacher from a setting where many people participated in the planning and carrying out of each day-care day. I was not disappointed.

In response to my questioning, Maria was able to explain to me the beliefs that shaped her program as well as her own feelings about her work. Because Spanish was her primary language, she had few English clichés at her disposal. This meant that each answer had to be freshly thought through. As a result she both illuminated the life in her infant/toddler room and enlarged my understanding of the whole day-care experience for children and for teachers. But before going on to Maria's own words I will fill out the picture with a few more details.

PROGRAM DESCRIPTION

This day-care center was located a short distance from a major city, but it was not in an affluent suburb. It was up among bare hills and shopping centers and small clusters of housing. Here, as in the Eastern urban center, there was an ethnic and socioeconomic mix in the groups of day-care children that came from the surrounding communities. Licensed and funded by the state of California, the center was operated by a nonprofit corporation. Parents paid on a sliding scale according to income. The doors were open from 6:30 A.M. to 6:30 P.M., and the center provided before- and after-school care in addition to its infant and preschool programs. Children from the ages of 3 months to 10 years were accepted at this center, priority being given to those families with the lowest income. At the time of my visits the center had one infant/toddler room that served eight children. However, I was told that there were 250 children on a waiting list for this group and the pressure was on to raise the number of children to at least 10.

Organizing Time

Together Maria and her assistant, Letty, had sole responsibility for a day that went from 7:30 in the morning to 5:00 in the afternoon. These youngest children were kept for a shorter period than the others because of their age. The slightly shortened time meant that either Maria or Letty was with the infants and toddlers during their entire day at the center. One teacher came early, one remained until five, and they arranged their schedules between themselves. Occasionally a staff member from one of the older groups down the hall, with a few moments to spare, would drop in to help, or to socialize with the teachers and babies, so the infants and toddlers got to be familiar with some of the other adults in the center.

Children's Ages

During the three weeks that I visited the program one child was moved to an older group and a 9-month-old baby was added in her place. After this move the regulars were two children 11 months old, three children 15 months old, one 13-month-old child, one child of 12 months, and the 9-month-old newcomer. Some of the children arrived after nine in the morning, some were picked up by four o'clock, and there were usually one or two absences, all of which made it just possible for the two teachers to cover the whole day every day.

Furnishings

The room was pleasant to be in because it had no apparent safety hazards, was flooded with natural light, never smelled of soiled diapers, and the floors looked clean and unspotted. Everything happened in this one space, including eating, sleeping, changing, and washing. In addition all the equipment was stored in the nursery—extra diapers, bedding, clothes, food, and toys. The size of the room was approximately 25 by 40 feet, with high windows along one wall and with a door opening directly onto an enclosed play yard that was shared by the whole center. Over half of the floor was a raised carpeted area; the rest was covered by linoleum on which the sink, the diaper-changing counter, and floor-to-ceiling storage cabinets were located. Cribs lined the other end of the room. Food preparation was on a shelf at one side with a small refrigerator and its own high cabinets.

No Privacy

Because none of these furnishings protruded into the room the middle was clear, giving the nursery a sense of openness with plenty of space to transform in various ways during a day. Another result of this arrangement was that all the children were in sight of both teachers all the time. I soon began to see, in spite of the lack of opportunities for privacy, that this visibility actually reduced teacher stress and increased safety in a room full of 1-year-olds where two teachers were responsible for everything that happened, and where at the beginning and the end of each day only one adult was present.

Play Materials

Small toys directly available to the toddlers were on two open shelves. There were in addition large wooden blocks to climb on, some plastic kiddie cars, and a wagon big enough to hold two children. The teachers had decorated the wall over the cribs with their own artwork; and down low where they could be touched were commercial nursery pictures designed to teach colors. Although this was not a very richly imaginative setting, it nevertheless was cheerful and quite flexible.

Schedule

The daily schedule, neatly printed and pinned to the wall, read as follows:

7:30 - Open the room. Inside free play.
8:30 - Breakfast.
9:00 - Clean up. Potty-diaper change.
9:15 - Educational activities. Physical activities. Science.
10:10 - Art.
10:30 - Outside activities.
11:00 - Cleanup. Lunch.
12:00 - Cleanup. Potty-diaper change.
12:30 to 3:30 - Nap time.
3:30 - Potty-diaper change.
3:45 - Snack.
4:00 - Cleanup. Music. Story time.
4:30 - Potty-diaper change. Inside/outside free play.
5:00 - Close room.

Negatives and Positives

I am describing all this in some detail to make it clear that I am not holding up this center, or Maria's program, as an ideal model. There were a number of things, both practical and theoretical, that ran counter to what I think would best serve 1-year-olds in day care. First, I do not believe that this kind of isolated program is desirable, even if gifted and energetic teachers are able to sustain it for a while. In fact, Maria told me when I left that she was looking for another job. Although she loved the work, the conditions were just too hard. As for the specifics of the children's day, many of these were also far from ideal. One example was the eating arrangement, which was difficult for teachers and socially blank for children. Nevertheless, I always enjoyed being in Maria's room. No matter how open to criticism some aspect of the program might be on the surface, there was usually a balancing factor that turned it into a positive.

For example, at these mealtimes the children were lined up in their high chairs too far apart to touch, and not in a position to make easy eye contact with each other or their teachers. Maria and Letty moved back and forth, focusing on food delivery with occasional instructions to the children such as, "Keep your food on the plate." This was definitely not a social time in any obvious sense. Yet there was a built-in positive that was significant. Each child got a warm, physically close moment with one of the teachers when picked up, both before the meal and afterwards. Maria often accompanied each lift not only with a hug but also with a swift kiss on the cheek.

Here was just one sample of Maria's behavior that overrode the parts of the program that were less than perfect for teachers, or for children. Something was happening that kept the children alert and responsive, which made this particular center feel like a good place for babies, a place that they clearly trusted. It was really what led me to ask Maria for an interview, and why in the next chapter I will describe and discuss some specific scenes from her nursery room.

INTERVIEW WITH MARIA

INTERVIEWER: How long have you been working with this very young age group?

MARIA: About 2 years. I was working with 3-year-olds before.

INTERVIEWER: Do you have a special plan for each day besides your schedule?

MARIA: Yes, I plan every week for the whole week. It's not just for one day, but for the whole week. I have my schedule, but it's not a routine. If the babies don't feel like working or doing something, I don't force them. It is mostly what they feel like doing or not doing. Sometimes they are not in the mood to do something and you cannot do anything with that. I put it in the schedule and I try to do it at the time I plan, but if they don't like it or they don't feel like doing it we change the time.

Actually I work from intuition, when I feel they want to see something, because they show what they feel or what they want. Then I have all these plans in my mind. For instance, when we are playing outside and we see a puppy or a cat passing by, then I show them the puppy or the cat and they enjoy it. We can hardly know all that we will do today, because if something happens and I have the chance to use it I will. Wherever I can do it, I show them.

When they're going to learn is the time I use, the best time for them, not for me. Because sometimes they feel like learning. Sometimes they want to see the goldfish. Even if it's not the time to teach it, I show them the fish because this is the time they're going to learn. When they want it, they learn more, not when I want it.

INTERVIEWER: When you talk about teaching, what do you mean? What do you think the children are learning from you right now?

MARIA:What we are working on now is body parts and colors. These are the things we are working on these days and these weeks, telling them about the body parts and telling them about the colors.

For teaching them to talk, I point to the body parts and the food they need. I repeat and repeat until they learn how to say what they want. For instance, if they want the bottle I say, "Do you want the bottle?" And I repeat *bottle* and *bottle* again until they know. Then after a few days they start saying it. Instead of just pointing, they say *bottle* or a sound that means bottle or water. I teach about things that are most important for them to know, that they need, like food, or the body parts in case they hurt, so they can touch the place or say what they want.

I am teaching the whole day here. It's not just when I'm making a circle and showing them words. I use everything I can. Even when I'm showing a little toy, I mention the name of the toy. "Do you want this toy?" When they want a little car, I say, "Do you want this car?" I am using the word *car* so they pick it up little by little. When they are eating is another time when we teach a lot. We teach them how to use the spoon, the cup, and mention all those words, so they're picking them up little by little. Pretty soon they know their own place, their chair, and how to wait. They learn to wait because sometimes we have to wait for the lunch to come to our room, and they learn to wait too. So I think the whole day is a teaching day, not only when we have a circle.

INTERVIEWER: What do you do about behavior that you feel is not acceptable? What do you do when one baby pulls another baby's hair?

MARIA: The best thing I can do is look at them eye to eye. I have to pick up the baby's attention with eye contact and tell him not to do it. "We don't do that with the baby. He's our FRIEND." I have to repeat two or three times to the baby, looking into his eyes. Then with the same eye contact, show him, "This is the way we treat the babies. We play friendly with them." And I teach him how to do it. It takes time but they learn. They learn it's not what they're supposed to do. They learn it's a No-No. We say, "It's a No-No." That reminds them they're not supposed to do it. No-No is a kind of cue for us. After a few times they just stop like that, because they know it's not acceptable.

INTERVIEWER: So you're teaching them language that helps them to meet your expectations?

MARIA: Well, sometimes, but not too much because we're supposed to teach them right. Sometimes we need to do things that help them learn, because hitting each other is really hard for them. Since they're babies, we have to use little cues. If we just *say* it, they don't understand. They don't even pay attention to us. They just run away.

INTERVIEWER: You have mentioned eye contact as important when you're teaching children not to hit. I've noticed that you and Letty are responding to the children's sounds and actions with eye contact all the time. Can you say why you do that?

MARIA: I think it's important even for adults. When you make eye contact with the person who is talking to you, you know that person is paying attention and you feel important to that person. The babies are really important, and they want to be important. People who don't pay too much attention to them because they are little babies think that they don't feel or understand. But they do understand when nobody cares. That's why they try to cry or throw things. That means they want attention. That's why they throw the milk, or they throw the bottle, or they pull somebody else's hair. They do that because they want some attention. This is the way they say, "Here I am and I want your attention."

INTERVIEWER: Do you think children this age get some nourishment from each other when they're in a group like yours? Do they care about each other?

MARIA: Yes, I think so, I'm positive they do. Each group is a kind of family. When they are with the 2-year-olds outside, it seems as if they protect each other from the older ones. They know their group is together. They know that they belong to the babies and the others belong to the other group.

Living together every day they learn how to love each other. They like each other and they play together. Sometimes they fight like all the kids. Brothers and sisters love each other a lot but still they fight, so I think it's like a family. They love each other and they know each other.

INTERVIEWER: Do you do anything that helps to create this feeling in your group?

MARIA: I'm trying to create a little home for them, so they can feel at home and at the same time they're learning. They are at school and at home at the same time. We teach them to take care of the other babies. Everybody is a baby, but the youngest one is *the* baby. So we say, "Take care of the baby." And they feel like they're big. They take care of the little ones. They are used to doing that, so they feel like brothers and sisters. They take care of each other. Even outside, when the older group comes, if someone tries to do something to the baby, they say "The baby! The baby!" So they understand that we take care of each other.

INTERVIEWER: You have described a number of techniques that you use in your work with the babies. Do you think that caring for this very young age group is different from working with older children?

MARIA: Working with babies is really hard. I worked before with 3-year-olds in Mexico, but working with babies is hard because you have to have a lot of intuition to know what they want, because they don't talk. You have to see their reactions. You have to think what they want. A lot of times you have to guess what is going to be better for them. Sometimes they want to play. Sometimes they just want to be calmed down, and you have to guess because they don't know. You have to learn their language. When they ask me for something, now I know. But it takes time to learn to work with babies. That's my opinion. It's hard.

INTERVIEWER: Are you saying that you have to learn to read their body language?

MARIA: Yes, maybe. I have a lot of feelings for what the babies need when they need it. Sometimes you just feel that the only thing they need is a big hug, and then they run away because they're satisfied with it. That's what they wanted. Just like when they want some water and you give some water to them and they have the water and then they go play. Sometimes they just want a hug or a kiss. Then they go play.

INTERVIEWER: When I was here last week after naps, the children all began to cry at once. When you gave them each a drink of water, they stopped. How do you know what the babies' cries mean?

MARIA: It's paying a lot of attention, I think. If you put your attention on them every day the way I do, you learn what they want. You get a feeling from the cry or the way they're acting. Now, even though they're not talking, they know how to express to me when they want something. You notice sometimes when they want to see the goldfish, they go and look up at the fish? Even when the fishbowl is next to the sink, I know it is the fish they want. I know when they want water and when they want the fish. It's different for me. Even though it's in the same place, I know what they want. But I cannot explain because it's inside of me. It's just being here every day.

INTERVIEWER: Children under 2 are apt to cry a lot. What are your feelings about that? What do you do about it?

MARIA: It depends what they are crying for. If they are crying for fussing, I can talk to them. Sometimes I even put them in time-out by sitting them in a corner so they can come back by themselves and play again. Sometimes they just need a hug and love. Sometimes they cry because they hurt, so I can do something about that. If they have a bump or a cut I put something on the place, and then some love too. Always love!

INTERVIEWER: Can you hear the difference between different cries?

MARIA: Yes, that's what I mean when I say that it depends what's happening. The babies cry differently when they are hurt than when they are just fussing. It's really different. You can tell. When they are asking for something, the cry is not deep. It's not the same as when they get hurt. Besides, when they get hurt I know, because I'm here and I'm watching them. So when nothing is wrong, I can see it. I always keep an eye on them.

INTERVIEWER: Now I want to ask you about touching. Do you think babies need more physical contact with their care givers than older children might require?

MARIA: To me it's important. I like to hug them and I like to stay near by them and sit with them. It's important because love is something you have to show them. They're so little, if you just say to them, "I love you," they don't understand you. So for them it's important that you show them that you care and that you love them. That's why I hug them. They feel it because it *is* something.

I have the feeling that babies and little kids have an extra sense for the people who really love them. For example, if one person comes to a baby and wants just to show the other person that he loves the baby, but if that person is not feeling it, the baby is going to turn away. They reject the person that doesn't love them. I know the feeling the babies have. If you don't care about them, they're not going to be with you. That's my experience. They have a feeling when someone is really taking care.

INTERVIEWER: What do you think is most important for these babies? What do they need most from their day with you?

MARIA: For me the most important thing is love, and love means care. So I love them and I take care of them. I take care of the necessities. These are to be clean, to be fed, and to be loved. They need a lot of love. They come and hug me or hug Letty. They love to be hugged. They like to be dancing and have someone to pay attention to them. That's why they do something and they take a look at you to see if you're seeing what they are doing. Even when they are dancing, they're watching you to see if you are paying attention. That means they want to be loved. They want to be important to someone else.

This job is more than changing diapers. I think it's the base for these little babies. When they grow up, they will have a good feeling, a good base of love. They will have something to give. They shouldn't start with problems. They should start with love and good care. They have to start with something positive. For them it is a hard problem if we do nothing but just change their diapers and feed them and didn't care about them. They're not going to have anything, not even if they're clean and if they're fed. They're not going to have anything to give, because it's nothing. It's not a base.

INTERVIEWER: What would be the maximum number of children per adult that would still enable you to give this kind of care?

MARIA: The maximum I'd say for being a really good, good teacher is three for one person. That's beautiful. You can do a lot of things. More than four babies to an adult is too much. You can hardly work with five babies for one person. Because they need a lot of attention and a lot of love and for giving all these things you have to be calm. When five babies are crying at the same time you cannot be calm. You cannot be yourself.

For me the best number is three babies to one teacher. You have the time and you have the strength to pay attention to three babies. Four or five is too hard for you. When you're so tired, you don't have the strength to work as much, and I like to work. I like to teach them. It's a satisfaction when you see them doing what you teach. When there are too many, you can't do it. They start crying or fighting and you have to put your attention to other things, not on the teaching. That's hard for me. I say that three to one is best.

INTERVIEWER: I'm interested in the easy way you and Letty work together. What can you tell me about that?

MARIA: Well, I've said this a lot, but it's the most important thing. There is a lot of love in Letty and me. We try to understand each other's problems. We help each other. We don't let our problems interfere with the babies, because we know it's not the babies' fault if we have troubles at home or wherever. Letty and I, we're really good friends. Sometimes she's doing most of the job because I feel depressed. Or I have some problem and I cannot work as much as I can when I'm healthy. She helps me and I do the same for her. If you understand each other, that's a kind of cooperation. It's the best thing to do for the babies. And Letty has a big heart too. That's the main thing.

INTERVIEWER: I need hardly ask you if you like your work.

MARIA: Oh, I love my work. I just love it. It's beautiful work. But you need to love your job to do it, because it's a hard job.

INTERVIEWER: Some people might think it was boring. Do you ever get bored?

MARIA: No, you don't have time to get bored. You never get bored. You have a lot of happiness. You have a lot of tiredness. You have a lot of fun too. So you don't have time to get bored. During their nap you need to be resting a little bit, because by then you are tired. So you have time for your plan sheet, or art, or to think what you have to do next day. No, I can't say that it's boring. I get tired. Sometimes I fret because I can't get all the things I want for the babies. But boring? No.

INTERVIEWER: Do you think what you're doing is important?

MARIA: Yes, I think so. I think I am doing something good for people, little people. I feel satisfied with my work because I love it and I'm trying to do my best. I think I'm doing something for these kids. Someday they are going to be grown up. They are going to have had something in their life when they were little, even though they'll never know me when they're grown. But I know I give this love when they need it, because their parents are working and cannot be with them the whole day. Nobody is going to notice, not even the babies, because they're so little. They're going to forget about me. But I know I give this love for them. That is something really nice for me to know.

OTHER VOICES

The voices of teachers like Maria are increasingly being recorded in books that try to uncover the ingredients of good child care. Attitudes and emotional resources that guide teacher behavior with children are illuminated by their own words. For example, William Ayers (1989) in *The Good Preschool Teacher: Six Teachers Reflect on Their Lives,* after extensive interviews with Anna, concludes, "Anna can remember and relive being a baby and a child. . . . Successful teachers remember. . . . They have the capacity to look at things as a child sees them" (p. 24).

Summing up what he learned from another teacher, Ayers writes, ". . . when asked to list the adjectives that best describe her as a teacher, Michele included four that would have been on my list and a fifth that was a surprise: nurturing, stimulating, calm, quiet, unsatisfied. She strives for something more" (p. 95). Here he is not referring to a discussion of money and recognition but to the teacher's awareness that there is always more to learn, and more improvement to be made in her skills. In my experience this is a feeling common to many day-care teachers, including Maria.

Teacher interviews also point up the connections between the nursery and the wider world of ideas, historical and philosophical. For instance, Maria had the idea of making a family-style learning environment in her infant room by trying to create a little age differentiation among her babies. It is interesting to note that Maria Montessori also wanted a range of ages in her groups. In *A Montes-*

sori Handbook, R.C. Orem (1966) says that Montessori thought "that an age range of at least three years within a class enhances the learning situation" (p. 172).

Taking this idea still further, Urie Bronfenbrenner (1972) in *Two Worlds of Childhood: U.S. and U.S.S.R.* speculates that we have something to gain by multi-age groups, but more importantly than that, we have much to lose by our present practices of segregation by age. He writes, "American society emerges as one that gives decreasing prominence to the family as a socializing agent" (p. 99). Then he points out that "from preschool days onward a child's contacts with other children in school, camp, and neighborhood tend to be limited to youngsters of his own age and social background" (p. 100). He goes on to say,

> The segregation is not confined to the young. Increasingly . . . social life becomes organized on a similar basis, with the result that, at all levels, contacts become limited to persons of one's own age and station. In short, we are coming to live in a society that is segregated not only by race and class, but also by age." (p. 100)

As more and more of our children are brought up in groups from their earliest years, Bronfenbrenner's words open an important discussion. For instance, could we make day care more homelike and varied by making it less rigidly segregated by age?

8 Three Kinds of Learning
Cognitive, Social, and Emotional

It is easier to decide *what* to teach children at different ages and stages in their first years than to come to a widely accepted understanding of *how* to teach children what we want them to learn. Maria's comments in Chapter 7, along with her actual program, serve as a dramatic resource for examining the kind of learning that can take place even in the youngest groups. So this chapter will describe several of her planned projects and discuss some of her teaching behaviors, in order to raise issues that I believe are central to learning for all children who spend their time in day-care environments. These issues revolve around three kinds of learning—cognitive, social, and emotional—that are prominent in the healthy development of young children.

COGNITIVE LEARNING

Cognitive learning is influenced by the way teachers use time, the way they give praise, and how they ask questions in day care, and by their problem-solving techniques. Also, the very language used to talk about day-care programming shapes teachers' expectations of the children, and of themselves. Although these are only some of the aspects of teaching, they are ones that have a large impact on *how* teachers teach and *what* children learn.

Maria's Program

The schedule. Maria's schedule and the way she planned her time immediately aroused my curiosity. Was this her response to current studies about the importance of early learning? Was she trying to run her program like a first grade? What I discovered was quite the reverse. The parts of her schedule that were not necessary routines were flexible, largely child-directed as to duration, and often spontaneous as to times. The moments when the babies were not occupied with some business of their own were the moments when Maria introduced the curriculum part of her schedule. These teaching sessions provided some of the same elements that a home child might get from a trip to the grocery, or a visit to a friend's house. They injected new material into the day, along with a change of mood and tempo for children and teachers alike.

During my visits to Maria's nursery room I came to understand another aspect of her complicated schedule. Prescribed activities such as science, art, and music, which might be criticized as foolishly formal for babies, were a support for Maria. She used the curriculum written into her daily schedule as a technique to give shape and variation to what otherwise might have seemed to her like endless hours and days of physical baby care. She said she never got bored, and I believe one reason for this was her constant planning. It gave her the intellectual stimulation she needed to keep alert. She thought about activities she would like to try with the children. She identified concepts and skills she wanted to teach them. As a result, every day had a purpose beyond simply juggling the logistics of diapers, meals, and naps.

Structure.   Along with the support it gave her, Maria's schedule reflects the commonly held belief that babies and young children need structure and predictability in their lives. Though individual families differ widely on this subject, none of them would dispute the fact that this age group does need to feel safe when away from home, and that predictable events help to fill their need.

Nevertheless, it is worth remembering that babies start out living in a world without clocks, other than their own biological ones. When teachers talk about the need of babies and children for structure, they also may be saying that they themselves need structure.

During the process of acculturation, young children adjust their own rhythms to get in step with the adult world. Although this starts at home with the intensely personal exchanges between parents and infants, it necessarily becomes part of every day-care program. Teachers like Maria and Letty could hardly sustain such long hours without developing a schedule.

Of course, this adult need for structure can also result in inflexibility, and if structures grow too rigid, they overwhelm learning. Maria's structure, however, appeared to work in positive ways. With the following scenes, drawn from her program, I will try to make some of the intangibles of good teaching more visible. By intangibles I mean Maria's own behaviors toward, and interactions with, the children, which made each planned activity meet their needs as well as her own.

The Behaviors of Teaching

Making rattles.   One morning Maria was sitting on the floor greeting the babies as they came. It was a period of quiet adjustment from home care to center care. Maria kept her good-morning greeting to each child warm and short. While she spoke to the mothers, she did not leave the children but remained on the floor with them. As soon as the parents had gone, she focused on making a rattle out of a hinged plastic box just big enough to hold a small wooden block. She took the box, put a block inside, shook it next to her ear, and handed it to 16-month-old Max. All of the three children present were clustered around her knees watching. Max tried to open the box, could not, and handed it back to Maria. She accepted it without comment and showed again how it opened. Max reached out and took it back. This time, with a little physical help from Maria, he succeeded. Maria responded with her characteristic "Yeah!" that she always gave when a child had mastered some problem.

While Max continued to open and close the box and take the block in and out, Maria made a similar rattle for Richie, now eager to have one. By this time Duane, having cried when his mother first left, began to show some interest, his attention slowly drawn to the box-and-block activity. When he started to reach for Richie's box, Maria had a rattle ready for him too. This box-block challenge was an example of what she called children's *work*. Her role was to interest the children in a problem, then help them to solve it as much as was necessary. And, as always, timing was critical. Maria knew how to keep from rushing in too soon or holding back too long. Her concept of teaching also included giving praise for persistence and success.

Praise. Here I would like to make some observations in praise of praise. By praise I mean positive rather than negative responses to children's projects, ideas, and efforts, even when they may need some redirection. Rather than saying to Max, "No, you do it," when he handed her the box and block, Maria helped him to put it together, then underlined the result with her exclamation of pleasure.

Unfortunately praise has become a rather suspect behavior in many preschool circles, yet when a baby at home takes his first step, who would ignore him on the theory that this was expected behavior and therefore not praiseworthy? Or who would voice disappointment when he failed to walk across the room? The baby gets hugs and cheers and goes on to try again. Other kinds of learning may be just as necessary but are more easily discouraged, for example, when a teacher provides an idea and then withholds help, or tries to guide the child with negatives, as by saying, "No, that's not the way." Max might have thrown away the box if given no help, or lost interest if given no encouragement. He might even have done well on his own. Maria's praise did not detract from his learning. Instead, her pleasure appeared to add to his enjoyment by giving value to what he did.

Adults sometimes fear that undeserved praise or overpraise may actually destroy a child's incentive. Even though I understand this concern, I think withholding praise can be more harmful than helpful when applied to the youngest children. Actually I have never seen a teacher in day care nonsensically or absentmindedly doling out praise. Unfortunately the reverse is sometimes true, with teachers withholding praise or giving approval grudgingly, as though they felt it was somehow bad for a child to have his or her achievements responded to with warmth.

Basically preschool children want the approval of their primary care givers, teachers and parents. Maybe in a deep biological sense they are aware of the dependency that can make approval of primary adults a life-and-death matter. When a care giver withholds praise, many accomplishments not only go unacknowledged but unrecognized even by the children themselves. How can young children necessarily know when they are on the right track to gain adult approval if no adult approval is shown?

Besides serving as a guidepost and reassurance, praise makes children feel good about themselves. Overpraising, even if it should occur in a day-care situation, is far less likely to dim a child's enthusiasm than the opposite, the absence of approval with the accompanying feelings of being in an unfriendly, incomprehensible environment.

It is almost axiomatic that a teacher who enjoys children, and hasn't suppressed expressions of this enjoyment, will have a teaching style that includes more positives than negatives, more praise than criticism. If praise should become automatic or undeserved, children will soon let it be known, for they are quick to pick up what is false or insincere in adult behavior and language, and will turn away. But any confusions arising from false praise are a trifle, compared with the serious loss of incentive for the child who has little approval. Every child needs to feel early, and often, the satisfaction and pleasure of achievement.

Circle time. Another scene demonstrating Maria's use of timing and praise took place one morning when she saw that the children were ready for attention. Their aimlessness was her cue to sit down on the floor with a book in her hand and call for them to come. It became the story time on her schedule, or what she called "circle." Because Maria was the dramatic and emotional center of the room, around whom interesting things were sure to happen, the boys and girls looked glad to gather, although some were led or carried over by Letty, and others showed no interest in the book itself.

This time Maria had chosen a book with large photographs of individual body parts. The pictures that she selected to show were of a head, neck, arm, and hand. Although the children responded to the head and hand pictures, the neck and arm were incomprehensible. In a fashion that was typical of her trial-and-error method, Maria took her lead from the children and focused on the pictures that interested them. Touching her head, she said, "Head. This is my head." She moved her hand from the picture to her head, then from the picture to each child's head, repeating the words, "Head.

This is your head." She concentrated on getting them to look, listen, and touch. Some of the children started touching their own heads, and each time this happened Maria would respond instantly by using the child's name, saying something like, "Good, Liza! That is your head." Whatever the individual children were learning from all this, Maria's delight in the responses she got made her praise a general celebration that was shared by everyone.

When the hand picture came up, 12-month-old Andrew had had enough of just looking at the pictures and wanted to touch them. With the briefest hesitation, Maria switched from holding up the picture to holding it out. The children crept closer and closer until they had overwhelmed the book with their hands and knees. Instead of trying to prolong the session, Maria simply laughed. Handing the book to Letty, she freed her arms to give brief hugs and to play with each child who had crawled over the book to reach her. When I looked at my watch, only 3 minutes had passed.

Teaching by giving.   In the simplest sense, to teach another person successfully is to give them something. One accepted method for doing this in day care is to gather all the children together in a group to learn from their teacher. Although preschool teachers try to give information, insights, concepts, and skills during these sessions, the behavior some slip into is not *giving* behavior. Instead they get stuck in a kind of *questioning* behavior. The result is a teaching-by-testing approach that is just the opposite of giving out something that will be valuable to the children, or pleasurable.

There are, of course, *giving* questions that open up possibilities, ones that give children an opportunity to share what they know without being limited to a single answer that the teacher wants. "Would anyone like to tell what they had for breakfast?" is a giving type of question. But, "What is the name of this animal?" is not a giving question unless the teacher is sure that every child knows the answer.

It is interesting to speculate on this tendency to ask endless questions of young children. Parents spontaneously start asking questions of babies right from birth. They ask questions and answer them themselves to stimulate and to elicit response. "Are you smiling? Yes, you are." They ask questions when giving soothing verbal replies to infant crying. "Here I am. Did that thunder scare you?" Later they ask questions as a way of giving choices, so that young children can begin to experience a little bit of control over their own lives. "Do you want some milk on your Jello?"

In fact, parents, and care givers generally, ask questions of young children for all sorts of *giving* reasons before they expect any answers. These are questions to show interest, to show concern, to show respect, and to show love. However, both parents and teachers often forget how to read the behavioral messages of preschool children when these children learn to talk. Instead, questions tend to stop being used in *giving* ways once a verbal answer can be expected. This is a dramatic, unintended contradiction that can be seen in many day-care circle times. I believe one reason for this is the need to control. For example, if a teacher wants to teach the days of the week to a group of 3- or 4-year-olds, and she tries to do this by keeping them focused on her and sitting still, questions can sometimes help her. They do interest children for all the positive reasons I have listed. Questions suggest a drama, a social exchange, an opportunity, but if used primarily to control, they can become increasingly hostile. When a teacher asks the child, who does not know the days of the week, what day it is in order to stop her talking to her friend, this is not a *giving* question. So it is important to understand just how questions are being used in different situations, that is, to understand when they are an effective teaching behavior, and when are they intended for purposes other than teaching, with possible negative results.

The children in Maria's infant/toddler group, who had only a few beginning words, were on the developmental fulcrum in between not being expected to answer questions, and being questioned in order to be taught. In spite of her experience with an older age group, Maria taught by giving answers rather than asking for them during her circle time. The rattle-box episode was also a clear, step-by-step demonstration of teaching by giving. Although Maria was interacting with 1-year-olds, the same *giving* behavior can be used for teaching 2s, 3s, and 4s, if modified to fit the different levels of maturity.

Questions are not necessary to teach young children in groups, or singly, and I believe it is better that they not be used at all rather than overused or misused. Of course, adults ask questions all the time when they are around children, teachers being no exception. It is not the innocuous questions that I am referring to but the ones that actively promote learning, or inhibit it.

Finger paints.   In this next vignette, Maria's plan went totally awry. She had decided to introduce her group to finger paints, but the project was not well planned. There were six toddlers seated around one small table. The children were too crowded. The papers were too small and were not fastened down. Maria and Letty tried to show the hesitant babies how to smear the gobs of green paint, with the result that the teachers' own hands were soon covered. At the same time they were trying to show the babies how to keep their hands on the papers and the papers on the table. It was all too complex. Although every child was protected by a smock, a smock will not cover the critical parts of a 1-year-old. Soon they began to get paint on their faces, in their hair, and it looked as though their eyes would be next. At this juncture Maria and Letty, with one communicating glance, moved into a superefficient cleanup operation. In terms of purely physical management it was a crisis. One by one the children were whisked onto the changing counter to be wiped off, then put temporarily into their cribs away from the paint. Naturally the children did not like the wiping, and appeared generally bewildered by the rapid turn of events. For the teachers this fiasco meant a big increase in physical labor. However, the point of the story is that at no time, either by voice or body language, did the teachers indicate that they thought the children were at fault. When 14-month-old Duane wandered away in his paint-covered state to leave his print on the carpet, both teachers called out to him at once, "Stay over here, Duane." "Hey, Duane, wait!" Their hands were full so they could not go to him immediately. When Maria finally did get to him, he appeared glad of her attentions, and she did not spoil this by saying, "Look what you did to the rug!" even though she was clearly upset with her failed project.

Maria was able to solve the physical problem that she herself had created without involving her group emotionally by blaming them. The children may have been bewildered, but they were not chastised.

Problem solving and flexibility.   Often in difficult social moments, the opposite of problem solving and flexibility is blame.

Maria's finger-painting session is a good example of a teacher who avoids this common pitfall of blaming the children when things go wrong. It may be easier to avoid *blaming* behavior with preverbal children than with older children. But even with 1-year-olds, there are times when a teacher who cannot understand or control a child or a situation feels hostile. Then, there is a tendency to find a formula that passes the teacher's responsibility on to the child, or perhaps a parent. A teacher might say, "That child never listens, so now look what happened to her," or "He pushes other children because his father plays so rough."

In such a situation it is important for all the adults involved to keep in mind how uneven development can be during these early years. If a child does not conform to the norm within a group, that does not necessarily mean that there is something wrong with either the child or the parents' child-rearing practices. A 3-year-old can behave like a 2-year-old one minute and like a 4- or 5-year-old the next.

I saw a good example of this behavior during a music session in a group of children older than Maria's. A teacher of 3-year-olds was playing a record to accompany marches and gallops, when one boy started to get wildly excited. He began going in the wrong direction and crashing into the other children. The teacher handled the transgression by stopping the music and briefly changing the format. She allowed this child, along with a couple of others who were interested, a chance to do solo gallops, which took much less control. When the next group gallop came, she had the wild galloper stay with her to turn over the record. This is what I mean by teaching with flexibility and with problem solving. The teacher was able to adjust the program to incorporate the more immature child without having to scold or blame. Later, in a discussion around the juice table, that same child had ideas that, in fact, did sound almost like those of a 5-year-old.

Blame, along with the kind of emotions it provokes, such as humiliation, resentment, and guilt, distracts children from one of their main tasks, which is to learn what is and is not acceptable, what does and does not work, and why. Just as in the episode of the screaming 3-year-olds in Chapter 2, children will learn a great deal from their own experience. What they need from their teachers is clarification, and support to behave in the desired way, without feeling diminished by the process of learning. Letting children know that some behavior is not acceptable, or that it is a very serious matter to disobey certain instructions, is not the same as blaming them. You can find comparatively strict teachers, who know how to be flexible in ways that incorporate a wide spectrum of developmental skills without making any child a *bad* child.

Interactions.   Ultimately it is the daily accumulation of small, nurturing interactions between teachers and children that determines the kind of experience the children will have in day care. Behaviors that lead children to feel positive about themselves and the world around them are what the successful preschool teachers have in common. This is at least a partial definition of good teaching.

The Language of Teaching

Problem words.   Because words influence how people think, a number of the words now used in day-care programming represent a problem, I believe. Maria's schedule, as well as her interview, calls attention to words like *work* and *educational activities*. The problem here has to do with formal learning. How much should be introduced in the nursery years, and how soon? Teachers have understandably shied away from the personalized language of home. They use fewer endearments as well as fewer harsh words. Their verbal guides are also more specific and consistent than is usual in a home. As a substitute for home words and styles of speech, teachers of preschool children have tended to step up the ladder to grade-school terminology. Grade-school terminology comes to be coupled in turn with grade-school methods of teaching. That can mean that preschoolers are expected to behave in ways that are not productive, such as the long periods of sitting still at table activities and circle times, or there may be too much emphasis on being quiet and listening to what the teacher says.

Work and play.   As a result, the word *work* is now in the day-care world, along with teacher dependence on table projects and structured materials akin to workbooks, while at the same time many programs have almost lost the important word *play*. Terms like *free play,* which usually means a choice of approved activities, *dramatic play,* and *water play* are in common use, but the word *play* by itself is not often recognized as representing a valuable activity. In fact, play behavior may be actually banned as nuisance behavior, unless it takes a prescribed form.

Because there is no generally accepted definition of the word *play,* it is as though it had been simply thrown out along with the mass of unscheduled child behaviors that it represents. This means that children's creative ideas, the ones unimagined by adults, often have no opportunities to develop in day-care centers. It is ironic that children who are away from home all day tend to be definitely more restricted in their free activities, and have fewer opportunities for play, than children in a shorter 3-hour nursery school.

The confusions of language.

The language of grade school has even begun to reach into infant/toddler programs, or at least into the ones that are not mostly baby-sitting places. Maria had her schedule with its educational activities, science, art, story time, and free play. Who would guess that her youngest charge was 9 months old? She talked about "circle." What did this mean in terms of infants and toddlers? She talked about babies "working," and she said she was "telling" them about body parts as though she might be giving them a verbal lesson in their biology.

Maria herself was never confused by these words, in terms of how she interacted with her children. She was only confused sometimes in terms of the methods and the content she chose in order to provide an enriching nursery life for them. However, I have seen other teachers who have been really confused, to the detriment of the children in their charge. For example, in one center that I visited, a group of 2-year-olds were kept at a table doing puzzles for 15 minutes until breakfast was served. Breakfast lasted for another 20 minutes. Both these times were pleasant enough, with talk back and forth between children and teacher. But then they were moved to the floor to sit in an orderly group, first to sing and then to listen to a story. During all this time, well over an hour, there had been no break, no freedom to move about, or separate, or choose activities. So before the story was finished several of the children tried to creep away to take books for themselves from the nearby bookshelf. At that point, when they were repeatedly stopped, a few of them began to cry. Here was a conscientious teacher more familiar with school *work* and scheduling than with nursery life and *play*.

SOCIAL LEARNING

For young children, cognitive learning also involves social and emotional learning. Like transparencies, these overlie each other almost completely, but I am going to separate them here in order to make a few more points about the nature of good child care.

One of the central differences between day care and home care is the fact of the group—a group that is usually all of almost the same age—and what young children learn through the group experience about themselves and others. The challenge for the teachers is how to manage in ways that nurture and guide the individual children within this social situation.

Values

Of course, the amount of attention children receive from teachers, the size of the group, and the teacher-to-child ratio all affect the quality of life for the individual. The level of education and the personal aptitude of the teacher also affect how well the individual child fares in a group. In addition, the adult values and assumptions about individual and group relationships play a role in shaping the experience of children in day care. As I described in Chapter 6, some programs focus on the individual child to such an extent that they largely ignore any positives that might be gained from the experience of group living. Other programs make the group the focus, training children to be able to move in concert at an early age but deemphasizing the individual at a point in life when identification of self is generally considered central to sound development.

The Group as a Family

Maria's program suggests a third alternative. She managed to make membership in her group a positive social experience even while she gave attention to the individuals in it. As she says in her interview, a nursery group has some resemblance to a family. That means that children who live together all day are not unlike brothers and sisters, who can and should care for each other. It was not that Maria expected infants and toddlers to be able to empathize. What she expected of them and tried to foster was that they be aware of each other as significant others, not just as objects or as a potential threat.

There were a number of ways that Maria went about building this feeling of group closeness. She made an effort to repeatedly call the individual children by name. This is a usual way to help children build their own identities in group situations, and become familiar with each other. Maria added to this level of awareness the message that there was a connection between the children. Just as young children have their own special teacher, they also have their own special group-mates, special because they are there.

Here is a concept often encouraged by parents but not always by teachers in day-care centers. However, Maria used every opportunity to teach the children that they were important to each other. For instance, when Max gave an experimental tug to Denise's hair, Maria personalized the other child for Max, modeling the desired behavior, rather than generalizing about hair pulling or scolding him for a bad act.

Another method she used to create a family kind of awareness in her group was occasionally to call or sing to all the children at once. In other centers I have often seen 3- and 4-year-old children addressed as a group only when being scolded. I suppose this can create a kind of group awareness, a brotherhood and sisterhood of chagrin. However, teachers who foster in young children a positive feeling for the group as a whole do it by using positives themselves.

One afternoon when Maria's children were all toddling and creeping around, having just been lifted out of their cribs after naps, two of the children began to cry. This general malaise was infectious, quickly spreading to everyone. I wondered what Maria would do. Letty was out of the room and it seemed an impossible situation. Maria, however, soothed them by handing each child a small paper cup of water. She accompanied this care giving with a cheering sing-song, "My babies. My babies," giving out the general message that they were all together and under her care, which meant that all was well. She bound the children to her and to each

other with her song. The message was understood. The babies
stopped crying, and Maria had time to pull up the shades and start
changing diapers and giving individual hugs, conversation, and eye
contact.

A Miniculture

Along with this awareness of significant others, there was a
second factor that made the group experience in Maria's room a
positive one. Like a home, her nursery had its own miniculture. It
was more than a waiting and learning place for babies while their
parents worked. There was a life for them during the day that had
some emotional tone and vividness, as well as some distinct physical
attributes. Maria's goldfish, her Spanish records, her circle times,
her way of moving and speaking all combined to give flavor to her
program, making it more nourishing, I believe, than a program that
was educationally correct but without style. The children shared
this miniculture, themselves becoming part of it. When Maria
called to them, they perked up as though wondering, "Now what
is she up to?" And because she always combined familiarity with a
modicum of surprise, her program appeared to be both reassuring
and stimulating to the children.

It would have been difficult to sustain this feeling of the group
as a supportive, caring unit if the staff had not been so continually
present. Rapid teacher turnover in day care is a serious problem for
children. But when a program fosters closeness to group-mates, has
a rich miniculture, and has a consistent teacher or teachers, the children can have a valuable social experience in group care. This does
not make day care better than home care, but it makes it a good
substitute for whatever some children under 5 may miss by spend-
ing so much time away from home.

Asking for Attention

Although the group itself can be a positive experience for preschoolers, that fact still does not address all the needs of the individuals in it. Maria had a clear solution to this problem with her

toddlers and babies. Everyone has heard adults who dismiss the behaviors of children with the words, "Oh, he just wants attention." Maria, on the other hand, actively encouraged her children to ask for her attention. Believing strongly that they needed her attention, and wanting them to feel that they deserved it, she was glad when they demanded it. This kept a running exchange going between her and the babies. Every contact did not have to be initiated by her when the children were demanding. It was the undemanding children who required the most effort, like Liza, a child from a Vietnamese family, who spoke little or no English. Liza never smiled or cried or came for hugs, which made it necessary for Maria to constantly remember to make a place for her in the group, both physically and verbally.

Even when the manner in which the children in Maria's program bid for attention was not acceptable, the bids themselves were never rejected. This did not mean that she always gave the children what they wanted, other than her attention. It did mean that she always responded to their communications. When she was at the changing table, for example, she might simply call across the room to a baby who was fussing to say that she heard him and was coming as soon as she could, which she invariably did. In another situation she might respond to a demand from a child by saying, "I am not getting the wagons out right now because———." In like fashion she reacted to the physical approaches of the children, first giving affection, then finding a project if the child did not find something on his or her own.

EMOTIONAL LEARNING

The emotional climate in group day care differs from that in parental care. Group living is inevitably not as intimate as home. Teachers do not ask, cannot ask, possibly should not try to ask, as much of babies as their parents do, in positive responses such as smiles and laughter. Babies, in turn, quickly learn to expect less in emotional response, and therefore to ask less of their teachers than of their parents. This should reassure parents who fear they are giving up their parental role.

The Feelings of Children

Intimacy.   In many programs it is startling to realize how serious the faces of infants and toddlers are. The kinds of games that parents play so regularly to provoke smiles and laughter are the exception, not the rule. Perhaps there is no time. Perhaps teachers feel that this kind of intimate interactive play is the province of parents, so they distance themselves from the children in this way in order to distinguish their behavior from that of family. In any case, teacher attention to infants and toddlers has less talking, joking, cooing, animated eye contact, finger waving, tickling kinds of play than that of the mother and father in almost any warm family. The method of keeping babies occupied, distracted, or interested, either alone or interacting with a teacher, is to focus largely on objects rather than on faces.

A definition of love.   Yet young children have some emotional needs that can and must be met in day care if they are to thrive. Primarily they need to trust their care givers. They need to feel safe in their human environment in order to reach out and explore the physical world around them with enthusiasm. Lacking the sense of a secure human contact during their hours away from home, infants and toddlers tend to droop. They go on "hold" with only brief periods of involvement, and some tune out the environment altogether. Maria was intensely aware of this danger. And I think her definition of what babies need from their teachers in order to thrive is the best that I have come across. When she said that babies need love, she defined love as care, care meaning more than simply attending to the basic necessities. Along with keeping the children safe, dry, and fed, a necessary teacher behavior is paying attention. Paying attention meant to Maria looking, hearing, making eye contact, and responding to the children's communications, including all their bids for attention.

Keeping in touch.   Finally, these infant/toddlers quite literally need to keep in touch with their teacher. In order to thrive they have to know that they can physically contact a primary care giver, and be confident that she will contact them from time to time. Here again Maria has a graphic definition of both the role of touching between teacher and child and of its limits. She explains with a simile, suggesting that touching can be just as matter of fact, while at the same time as life giving, as handing a young child a drink of water. A caring touch does not have to be synonymous with sensual intimacy or with prolonged hugs and kisses.

The Feelings of Teachers

"Nobody is going to notice."   I can hardly close this chapter without saying something about the feelings of teachers. It is a big responsibility to make an all-day life for young children, quite different from planning 2 or 3 hours of nursery school. For one thing, the reasons for the children's presence are different in these two situations. Parents often go to great lengths to send their children to nursery school a few hours a week, because they believe it is good for development. Parents and teachers would agree that some nursery school experience can be an enrichment for 3- and 4-year-olds, even 2-year-olds. On the other hand, children who spend a full day every day in day care are usually there to meet adult necessities rather than their own.

This puts a psychological burden on day-care teachers and the parents they serve. The nursery school teacher can feel proud that she is supplying something that is her unique contribution to enriching childhood. The day-care teacher, particularly of children under 3, can have no such confidence. (I am not discussing here the needs of children from inadequate homes.) Devoted teachers in most day-care centers may have confidence that they are giving the children in their care a good and enriching experience, but it is still viewed as a substitute for parental care.

Emotional commitment.   Nevertheless, a teacher can hardly communicate the kind of caring that will make the youngest children feel secure unless she makes a genuine emotional connection to them. The teacher who leaves herself open to feelings for the children is then open to the kind of involvement that parents have for their dependent offspring. The dependency of the children evokes a matching sense of responsibility from the caring teacher.

This is an emotional drain, which can be balanced only by the satisfaction of playing so needed a role in the lives of others, and by a real enjoyment of young children.

With each additional month and year, children become less dependent and thus elicit and need less of this type of emotional involvement. By the time they are 2-year-olds, the teacher's job has begun to shift to more complex social problem solving and curriculum planning. But, although the demands on the teacher may change, they do not shrink. Children in day care need a special commitment from their teachers that, because of the elusive nature of emotional learning, is not easily defined. In some of the ways I have discussed, Maria did define this commitment by the behaviors and attitudes visible in her program.

CONCLUSION

How children are responded to is more important, with more impact on learning, than the actual content of programs. Although the ways of teaching are difficult to standardize, because they are so shaped by individual interpretation, I am going to make a trial How-To list, compiled from my many hours of watching Maria and other skilled day-care teachers. Educators need to keep making these lists, and talking about them, until there is a more generally understood and widely accepted agreement on what teaching means in day care. The question always is, and will continue to be, how *do* young children best learn to learn? And how can their teachers help them? These are some of the ways:

1. Giving positive responses to children's positive achievements, both large and small.
2. Taking cues from children in deciding what to teach, and what they are ready to learn.
3. Teaching by giving as opposed to teaching by asking.
4. Learning and teaching the skills of problem solving rather than looking for a place to lay blame.
5. Teaching awareness of, interest in, and respect for others.
6. Respecting children's need for attention and valuing their ability to ask for it.

7. Gaining the trust of children by seeing and hearing and always responding thoughtfully to their communications.
8. Giving love, in Maria's sense, by caring enough about children to make the necessary commitment of time, energy, interest, and ultimate responsibility for their happiness and well-being away from home.

More discussion between teachers, directors, teachers of teachers, and parents about all the positive methods of learning and teaching would be an immediate way to start raising the amount of quality care in our day-care systems across the country. Michelangelo is supposed to have said, "Trifles make perfection but perfection is no trifle." Although perfection is definitely not the theme of this book, the importance of "trifles" is. Only by constantly returning to the minute, ongoing, give-and-take experiences of these youngest children can we identify with greater consistency what is essential for a good day-care experience.

OTHER VOICES

More than 10 years ago the Federal Government funded a major study of day care in this country, *Children at the Center: Summary Findings and their Implications* (1979). In a concrete way this report reflected our hopes for the future, which is now here. But it did not fulfill its promise. It showed an idealism about the care for children that we have not translated into action on a large scale. The fact that so little of what was projected as good care has materialized for children and families in need is discouraging.

Now a new study has been published, *Who Cares for America's Children? Child Care Policy for the 1990s* (1990). This was done under the auspices of the National Academy of Sciences by the National Research Council. It includes strong recommendations for government support and standards. These show that we do know where to start on child-care reform, that we do have creative ideas, and that we want to provide all our children, who must have day care, with a good start in life.

In addition, Congress finally passed child-care legislation in 1990, The Child Care and Development Block Grant, as well as expanding Title IV-A of the Social Security Act for the "At Risk" Child Care Program. Long overdue, this legislation is intended to help us state by state to aid young children, their families, and their teachers and child-care providers. But there are still questions to ask: How rapidly can we develop a wider understanding of the daily interactions and problems of child care at the local level? How effective and how widespread will our efforts be? And can we and will we now begin to improve the day-care experience for everyone's children?

Suggested Reading

These books that I have followed with a brief comment may be especially useful, with insights for teachers and parents about themselves and each other, and with informed descriptions of child development.

Ayers, W. (1989). *The good preschool teacher: Six teachers reflect on their lives.* New York: Teachers College Press.
> Through interviews and observations of their work, Ayers builds a portrait of each teacher. The separate age groups involved are of children 1 through 5.

Brazelton, T. B. (1983). *Infants and mothers: Differences in development* (2nd ed.). New York: Dell.
> The author describes three general types of babies—average, quiet, and active—an important concept for understanding babies and young children generally.

Bronfenbrenner, U. (1979). *The ecology of human development: Experiments by nature and design.* Cambridge, MA: Harvard University Press.
> Chapter 8 is a discussion of day care as seen through the medium of formal research.

Elkind, D. (1987). *Miseducation: Preschoolers at risk.* New York: Knopf.
> The author is deeply concerned about the pressures on young children to speed up, to learn more of those skills valued by adults faster and sooner.

Heffner, E. (1978). *Mothering*. New York: Doubleday.
    This book offers insight into how psychoanalytic theory and
    the women's movement shape the emotional experience of
    mothers and mothering.

Maynard, F. (1986). *The child care crisis: The thinking parent's guide
to daycare*. Ontario, Canada: Penguin Books.
    The author gives a thorough overview of the pros and cons of
    day care. The book has some disturbing messages, along with
    helpful advice for day-care parents.

Miller, J. A., & Weissman, S. (1986). *The parents' guide to day care:
Everything you need to know to find the best care for your child—and
make it happy, safe and problem-free from day to day*. New York: Bantam.
    A very concrete book of checklists, and useful information,
    with specific opinions about development.

Paley, V. G. (1984). *Boys and girls: Superheroes in the doll corner*. Chicago: University of Chicago Press.
    A teacher's dramatic narration of a year with her kindergarten
    group: what she saw, what she heard, how they changed, how
    she changed.

Spiro, M. E. (1965). *Children of the kibbutz: A study in child training
and personality*. New York: Schocken.
    This book describes an alternative cultural style of childrearing
    in detail along with the results.

Stern, D. (1977). *The first relationship: Infant and mother*. Cambridge, MA: Harvard University Press.
    The author discusses exactly how and why babies interact so-
    cially from the very beginning of their lives.

Tobin, J. J., Wu, D. W. H., & Davidson, D. H. (1989). *Preschool in
three cultures: Japan, China, and the United States*. New Haven, CT:
Yale University Press.
    Professionals and parents view video tapes of their own
    schools and those of other cultures and comment on what they
    see.

References

Ayers, W. (1989). *The good preschool teacher: Six teachers reflect on their lives.* New York: Teachers College Press.

Bradley, B. S. (1989). *Visions of infancy.* Cambridge, England: Polity Press.

Brazelton, T. B. (1983). *Infants and mothers: Differences in development* (2nd ed.). New York: Dell.

Bronfenbrenner, U. (1972). *Two worlds of childhood: U.S. and U.S.S.R.* New York: Simon and Schuster.

Bronfenbrenner, U. (1979). *The ecology of human development: Experiments by nature and design.* Cambridge, MA: Harvard University Press.

Csikszentmihalyi, M. (1982). *Beyond boredom and anxiety.* San Francisco: Jossey-Bass.

Elkind, D. (1987). *Miseducation: Preschoolers at risk.* New York: Knopf.

Hall, E. T. (1977). *Beyond culture.* Garden City, NY: Anchor Press/ Doubleday.

Hayes, C. D., Palmer, J. L., & Zaslow, M. J. (1990). *Who cares for America's children? Child care policy for the 1990s.* Washington, D.C.: National Academy Press.

Heffner, E. (1978). *Mothering.* New York: Doubleday.

Loftus, E. F. (1979). *Eyewitness testimony.* Cambridge, MA: Harvard University Press.

Maynard, F. (1986). *The child care crisis: The thinking parent's guide to day-care.* Ontario, Canada: Penguin Books.

Miller, J. A., & Weissman, S. (1986). *The parents' guide to day care: Everything you need to know to find the best care for your child—and make it happy, safe and problem-free from day to day.* New York: Bantam.

Orem, R. C. (1966). *A Montessori handbook.* New York: Capricorn Books.

Paley, V. G. (1984). *Boys and girls: Superheroes in the doll corner.* Chicago: University of Chicago Press.

Ruopp, R., Travers, J., Glantz, F., & Craig, C. (1979). *Children at the Center: Summary findings and their implications.* Cambridge, MA: Abt Associates.

Spiro, M. E. (1965) *Children of the kibbutz: A study in child training and personality.* New York: Schocken.

Stern, D. (1977). *The first relationship: Infant and mother.* Cambridge, MA: Harvard University Press.

Stern, D. (1990). *Diary of a baby.* New York: Basic Books.

Suransky, V. P. (1982). *The erosion of childhood.* Chicago: University of Chicago Press.

Tobin, J. J., Wu, D. W. H., & Davidson, D. H. (1989). *Preschool in three cultures: Japan, China, and the United States.* New Haven, CT: Yale University Press.

INDEX

About the Author

Elizabeth Balliett Platt, teacher and educational filmmaker, has a B.A. from Radcliffe College and a M.S.Ed. from Bank Street College of Education. During the 1960s and 1970s she was involved in starting therapeutic nurseries, first at Harlem Hospital and then at The New York Hospital, where she continued for 10 years as co-director and teacher in the Nursery School Treatment Center, Payne Whitney Clinic. During the past 10 years she has been filming and observing in day-care centers across the U.S.A. and in Europe, using her experimental films for workshops and lectures, and collecting material for this book. She has four young grandchildren and currently lives in Cambridge, Massachusetts.